DOUGLAS REMEMBERED

Cover photograph.

This photograph captures the feeling of the 1930's so well. Sadly, the incline railway, the amusement arcade, and the 'white' boats are no more. All the other ships in the picture are also long gone.

(Courtesy of Alan Kelly, Mannin Collections Ltd.)

II

It is not the person with little, who is poor,

but he that desires more.

Manx proverb

The Author

Douglas Remembered

By

Allan B Gill

ISBN No. 0-9537654-0-7

Published by: Mr. A. Gill, Burton-on-Trent, England.

Printed by: Nelson Press Co. Ltd. Douglas, Isle of Man, IM1 3LY.

Photographic Material

Most of the photographic material used is my own property. However, I am anxious to include several other photographs as well, and the search for them brought me into contact with people who were most kind, and pleased to help wherever possible. So it is with pleasure and sincere thanks, that the help and co-operation of the following organisations and individuals is acknowledged.

The Manx National Heritage

Bass Museum, Burton upon Trent

Heron and Brearley, Ltd.

Miss Hazel Hawley

Terry Faragher (The Terry Faragher Collection)

Peter Kelly

Alan Kelly (Mannin Collections Ltd)

Dedicated to

Laura, Emma and Alison

ACKNOWLEDGEMENTS

I have had valuable help from several people whilst preparing the manuscript, who have jogged my memory and filled in blanks. In particular I wish to thank my wife, Pat, for her help. In addition, I am indebted to Terry Cringle and Deemster Callow for their kind and helpful comments. The Deemster has also been kind enough to write the Foreword, for which I am most grateful.

Earlier this year, I spent a pleasant couple of hours with Ken Quane and David Byrne, reminiscing about the time when we all lived in Hillside Avenue. This refreshed my memories of the period, and enabled me to add to the relevant sections in the book.

My son, Quintin, deserves a special mention, for it is through his enthusiasm and encouragement that the book has been published - the original intention was merely to present the manuscript to my grandchildren as a gift. In addition, Quintin seems to know many people who have been kind enough to make suggestions and offer helpful advice. Some of them are strangers to me, but to all of them, I say 'thank you'.

Last, but not least, my appreciation goes to Quintin's wife, Joy, for encouraging me to write the book, and to my three beautiful granddaughters who have made it such a worthwhile task.

Allan Gill

Burton-on-Trent, 1999.

FOREWORD

By His Honour
Henry Callow, C.B.E.

Allan Gill's clear memory of his schooldays and of events that happened in his childhood enables him to paint a vivid picture of Douglas in the 1930's. Discipline in school was strict and there was no Welfare State, but the visiting industry was flourishing, cinemas and dance halls were in their heyday, there were no parking problems and little crime.

This account should appeal not only to those who are of an age to recall the events and personalities the author describes so well, but also to younger readers who wish to learn what Douglas was like when it was a thriving tourist resort. I commend it to both groups, and hope they will enjoy it as much as I have.

Henry Callow.

CONTENTS

	Acknowledgements	VI
	Foreword	V II
	Introduction	
1	In the beginning	1
2	Schooldays	7
3	Twenty-eight Hillside Avenue	25
4	Playing, places and pastimes	59
5	Charities plus benefactors	95
6	Interesting people	103
7	Work	115
8	Wartime	133
9	Life in the RAF	155
10	Epilogue	209

INTRODUCTION

I always listened with interest whenever my father talked to me about old Douglas. It seemed incredible that so many changes had taken place since he was a boy living in that part of the town that is now occupied by the Lord Street bus station and its surrounds. In those days it was the heart of the town, with places such as Parade Street, New Bond Street, Big Well Street and Seneschel Lane. My grandparents lived in 6, Drury Lane, a fine house that had belonged to the Duke of Athol, before he moved to Castle Mona.

Meanwhile, the tourist industry was growing, so lots of new houses were being built on the promenade. My grandfather's brother, Alexander Gill, built many of them. My father worked for him on some of these fine houses, and Dad often reminisced about the people, events, places and life of the period. I wish that I had written it all down, as I now have no clear recollection of much of what he told me, so something precious to me is now lost beyond recall.

I have three beautiful grandchildren, and it occurs to me that when they are older they may be interested in the world in which I grew up, for it will be as strange to them as my father's is to me. Also, as I lived through the war years, I have indulged in a few reminiscences of my time in the R A F, in the hope that it may be of some interest.

One of the nice things about the time that I was young is that there was a distinct division between the stages of growing up. Children were innocent creatures, and treated as such until they were about fourteen. Then came that wonderful period of adolescence, a time of discovery and gentle transition to the adult world. We had very little money, so were not a target for commercial exploitation as now. In fact, the whole system was geared to adults. Thus, there was no separation of older and younger people in the main leisure and entertainment worlds - we all went to the same cinemas and dance halls, listened to the same wireless programmes, and generally we served our apprenticeship for adult life. This was a vital part of the growing-up process in which we were obliged to adopt the social mores of the adults. It bore not the slightest resemblance to the situation today, when it often appears that even very young people are mini-adults, have their own music, clubs and, in fact, seem to live in a world from which adults are excluded. This seems to be particularly so in Britain. I don't say it is better or worse, but it is certainly different.

Violence was almost unknown, drug-taking non-existent, easy sex very rare (the girls preferring to take no chances, rather than run the risk of getting pregnant before marriage). Bad language was rarely heard in public, and never in the presence of girls, and there was complete respect for other people's property. In short, it was, in my opinion, a very civilised society, where standards were clearly defined and rigidly maintained.

Another of the differences between then and now is that most people could not afford to travel very far. One holiday a year in places such as Blackpool or, if you had more money, the Isle of Man, was normally the most to which working people from Britain could aspire. In 1931 the single saloon boat fare to the Island from Liverpool, Heysham or Fleetwood was thirteen shillings and sixpence (67p). A trip to London was beyond the means of most workers in the north, even though rail fares were less than a penny (1/2 p) a mile.

In the Isle of Man a room in a promenade boarding house cost 2/6d a day for bed and breakfast. Thus, when calling housey-housey (bingo) numbers, 26 (i.e., two and six) was always called as 'bed and breakfast'. Full board cost 7/6d a day. At that time, there were four US dollars to the pound, so five shillings was referred to as a dollar.

As I have not lived on the Isle of Man since 1950 I must rely on my memory for some of the names, places and so on. Therefore, I trust that I will be forgiven for the inadvertent errors that must surely have found their way into the text, despite my best endeavours. I only hope that they are few in number.

My youngest son, his wife, Joy, and their three young daughters live in Port St. Mary, so perhaps one day one of them will write a follow-up story, about life as it is now. On my visits 'home', I am struck by the changes in Douglas since my boyhood days. I, and many of the children that I played with, would now be described as 'disadvantaged'. In our day, though, nobody told us, so we carried on enjoying life in cheerful ignorance of our sorry state. In fact, we were all quite sure that we were having a wonderful time and, like me, I am confident that they still think so.

But how swiftly those childhood days passed. It seemed that they would go on and on, but quietly and gently they faded away like a beautiful sunset, gone forever. T E Brown summed it up so eloquently and evocatively when he wrote:

> '.... And when you look back it's all like a puff,
> Happy and over and short enough.'

And now, as we move into the new Millennium, the pace of change is already very fast, and I expect that it will be even faster in the future. Places such as Douglas will, no doubt, continue to change out of recognition in many places over the next few years, but I hope that, whatever happens, it will remain a wonderful town in which the children can grow up in safety, and with many happy memories.

Allan Gill,

Burton-on-Trent, 1999.

CHAPTER ONE

IN THE BEGINNING

If wishes were horses, then beggars would ride.

The year 1925 was eventful in some ways:

Margaret Thatcher was born.

Hitler's Mien Kampf was published.

Christiana, the capital of Norway, was renamed Oslo.

On the thirteenth of June, I was born.

My birth took place in 16 Allan Street, Douglas, and I was called Allan (after Allan Street), Bennett (my mother's maiden name). I don't remember anything about the place where I was born, as my family moved into one of the new houses in Hillside Avenue, number twenty-eight, when I was just three weeks old.

It seems that I was a delicate child, having been born prematurely, the youngest of five children, and all boys. I was washed in olive oil and wrapped in cotton wool. My eldest brother was Ernie, followed by Harry, Charles and George, who was five years older than me, so I feel that my arrival must have come as something of a surprise to my parents. The only one of my brothers that I had any real involvement with was George, as the others were so much older. Both Ernie and Harry were married before I was three, and Charles when I was about ten. I have no recollection of Ernie's wedding, and only a few disconnected mental snapshots of Harry's, whose reception was held in twenty-six, Hillside Avenue. The semi-D's in the avenue were of two types, kitchen and parlour houses. The latter were regarded as much more 'posh' than the others, so it was a plus if you lived in one. I did not. However, number twenty-six was, and the sister of the bride lived there, so that is probably why the reception was held there. By happy chance, my family moved into that very house in 1942, but that is jumping ahead.

The families in the avenue tended to remain for some years, so there was only a trickle of newcomers. Thus, in this slow-changing world, it was easy to keep track of which family lived in which house. Pride and neatness was the order of the day. The front path to the gate at most houses was washed and London-stoned regularly. Applying London-stone to the cement gave the path a bright, white surface. Some homemakers just applied a border, whilst others covered the whole path, which was inhibiting if one was obliged to walk on the newly 'stoned area. Brasso was applied regularly to the brass fittings, such as the house number, doorknocker, and any other brass fixtures, such as a nameplate. Moreover, it was not just the outside that was spick and span. For example, the fire grate and the fire irons were kept shiny and black by the frequent application of Zebo polish. The fire oven had a steel hob, knob and door hinges, all kept highly polished, so the whole cooking range was a joy to behold. Therefore, although people with little money, in fact, many of whom were very poor, occupied the houses, they had considerable and justifiable pride in their neat and tidy homes.

The Gill family, c 1929. L to R: Charles, Harry, Mother, Uncle Ernest Bennett, Grandma, Grandpa Gill, Emmy Gill (nee Duggan). Front row: Self, Ernest (Sonny) Bennett, George. My brother, Ernie, is not shown, so he must have been the one who took the picture.

The breweries used others, besides the huge Shire horses. Here, a smaller horse pulls a decorated cart and its delightful passengers, for one of the many parades of the time.
(Courtesy Heron & Brearley)

Some of the occupants became very good friends, such as my parents with Rachel and Willie Cooile. However, friendly relations were established with all the people. Often, a neighbour would just tap on the back door, open it and walk in, if she wanted to talk to my parents. The insurance man would do the same when he came to collect the weekly payment, often whilst we were sitting down to a meal. It was a very casual world, although everyone took care not to overstep the bounds of propriety.

Horse-drawn traffic was common, although it was gradually being displaced during the 1930's. Wooden barrels of beer were delivered to the pubs in large dray carts, pulled by magnificent Shire horses, whilst breadcarts were pulled by immaculately turned-out horses that looked like thoroughbreds. Docile animals that were content to just move at a sedentary pace pulled the milk carts ñ often they knew the round so well, that they moved from stop to stop without any assistance from the driver. A corollary of the horse traffic, was the dash of some householder into the road to 'clear up' after a horse had done its 'business', as the manure could be put to good use.

Dogs roamed freely on the street, as licences were not required until the latter part of the 1930's. In many houses a dog was kept as part of the family - not for guarding, as that was unnecessary, but just for companionship. My parents had one for many years.

It will not be a surprise when I say that no one in the avenue owned a motor car - in fact, I can not remember anyone owning a motor cycle, even an old crock. For weddings, funerals and similar needs, everyone had to be ferried in hired vehicles. My parents always used those belonging to Alfie Corlett, in Peel Road, a charming man who always gave his customers good value for money.

CHAPTER TWO

SCHOOLDAYS

The happiest days of your life.

My first day at school is still a vivid memory. My mother took me to Tynwald Street Infants School when I was five. As I remember, I was neither apprehensive nor excited, but just accepted my new situation as a matter of course. I was handed over to the headmistress; a rather large and pleasant lady called Miss Goldsmith. Later, I was to envy her, as she owned a Flying Standard motor car, something that few people could afford. It was black, as almost all cars were, and I recall clearly the width indicator which was mounted on the front left mudguard. It consisted of a vertical, chromium-plated rod, about six inches long, topped with a red knob. It gave the driver an excellent indication of the position of the left-hand side of the vehicle. You never see them now.

I was allocated to my first teacher, Miss Bridson. All the female teachers in those days were unmarried. I sat next to a boy called 'Nana' Bridson, not a relative of the teacher, and after that first day, Nana disappeared from my life. School was a happy time. The teachers stood no nonsense, but they were always fair. They made the lessons interesting, and we children played happily together at playtimes.

Although there were no lessons that I hated during my time at Tynwald Street, some were preferable to others. At the bottom of the list was knitting. Why was it necessary to teach boys to knit? We were obliged to provide the tools ourselves, so my mother provided me with a pair of thick needles, about eight inches long. They were light blue, with dark blue knobs and I can still see them clearly. To complete the assignment she provided me with some ghastly canary-yellow wool.

Thus provided-for, I set about knitting a tie. It had reached about nine or ten inches in length before I was able to discard it, probably because I left the class. The tie took forever to make, and looked awful. Even in its short length its width varied greatly - in fact, it was a classic piece of how-not-to-do-it knitting.

It was at this time that I confided to the girl sitting next to me that I had not had anything to eat at dinner time that day. (The mid-day meal was always called dinner). I was looking for sympathy, so I didn't tell her that I had gone home at dinner time as usual, but had been told-off by my mother for being cheeky. In retaliation I martyred myself by refusing to eat my dinner, and had returned to school in a haze of virtue, bad temper and hunger. I hoped to make some capital out of my martyrdom by getting her to sympathise with me, but instead she gleefully shrieked to the whole class, "Allan Gill hasn't had anything to eat today!" I forlornly shouted, "I have, I have! I've had a big dinner!" But it was too late - the damage was done. Even at this tender age I had learned how careful one must be when dealing with the opposite sex. I do not know what this little incident did to the impression the teacher, Miss Moore, had of my parents.

At eight years of age the girls transferred to Tynwald Street Girls School and the boys to Demesne Road Boys School. The one in Demesne Road was a small and pleasant place, and I think the building stands today just about as it did then. My first teacher was a very smart and good-looking young woman called Miss Brew. Each Friday we could bring a book from home to read during the last session of the day, and we all looked forward to this. There was always a good selection of reading matter in my house. It was mainly bought through Odhams Press offers in the Daily Herald, so I learned the joy of reading at a very early age.

For one of the Friday sessions, I brought a nicely bound and lavishly illustrated book called Wonders of the World. Each of the pictures had a detailed description intended for adult reading, so it was quite advanced for a child. Whilst I was studying the book Miss Brew was prowling round the class to see what we were reading. When she got to me she said, "You're not supposed to bring picture books. You're expected to read."
"But I am reading!"
She flicked the pages and stopped at a difficult caption.
"Read that." she demanded.
I did so without hesitation, so she told me that I could bring any books that I wished in the future. Miss Brew was a good teacher, and I was a bit sad when she was obliged to leave the teaching profession because she was getting married. Her husband-to-be was a member of the Felice' family who were well known in Douglas, as they owned a couple of very smart cafés in Strand Street.

It was whilst I was in this class that my mother allowed me to miss school one day to go with her to pick blackberries. The next day I solemnly presented Miss Brew with the note from my mother explaining how sick I had been the day before. Unfortunately, the effect was ruined by a little creep who proudly informed her where I had been. However, this was social suicide for him, as everyone hated a 'sleech'.

A woman called Miss White taught the next class. She was always called Ma White by us, as she was an older person. Mind you, one only had to be over twenty to be regarded as almost decrepit, an attitude that I do not suppose has changed with modern children. There were about thirty-three pupils in the class, and one of them was called Ted. One day he was called out to the front of the class for doing something wrong. I cannot remember whether he was to be caned or just told-off by Ma White, but whatever it was to be he launched a pre-emptive strike by kicking her on the ankle - hard. She let out a shriek and danced around the room on one leg, much to our amusement, although we dare not show it. Ted, with great presence of mind, promptly took to the hills. He rushed out of the classroom, out of the school and, we thought, out of our lives, for surely no one would dare to come back after doing such a thing? But no. The next day he was solemnly marched into school, made to apologise and given a good hiding. Even so, Ted remained a living legend for some time.

I enjoyed being in the school and did well. Usually Frank Harding and I shared the two top places in the class. Frank had an uncle who had ridden in the TT races, so he, Frank, was held in high esteem by the rest of us. His father owned a bicycle shop that stood on the corner of Drumgold Street. When aged eleven we 'sat' for the Douglas High School Entrance Examination. Both Frank and I were expected to pass without difficulty, but in the event, only he was accepted. Incidentally, it was the usual practice for parents to buy a bicycle for their talented offspring if he or she was successful. I, of course, did not qualify.

However, without Frank in the class I became the undisputed top boy in all the subsequent examinations during my time at school. One of the benefits of being the top boy was that I was automatically the one selected to be sent on errands. For example, when I was twelve I was in Dicky Cain's class, and each month I was sent to the branch of the Isle of Man Bank at the corner of Regent Street and

Strand Street to collect the staff wages. I carried a little attaché case for the money and, as this same procedure had been going on for years, the ritual must have been well known. However, I never felt in the slightest danger of being robbed and, as far as I know, the routine continued for years afterwards.

As I have already said, this was when I was in Form III, Dicky Cain's class. One day Ernie Murray did not turn up for school, so I was routinely selected to go to his house to find out why he had not come. His mother said that she could not understand what had happened, as Ernie had gone to school as usual that morning. It was obvious to me that in that case he was playing truant, but to cover for him I told his mother that probably it was his turn to go the woodwork class as some of the other boys had done. (The Woodwork Centre and the Central Gymnasium were located in the Art School building in Raphael Road). She was satisfied with this, but it left me with a dilemma - what would I tell Dicky? I decided to cover for Ernie, although we were not particularly good friends. Accordingly, I reported that Ernie was sick, and this was accepted without hesitation.

I did not give the matter another thought until, when I returned to the school after dinner, I found a large crowd of boys peering through the glass-panelled main doors. They were clearly watching something of considerable interest going on in the main hall. With some foreboding, I enquired what was happening. They were only too pleased to inform me that one of the boys was getting a good hiding from his father, because he and Ernie Murray had been playing truant. My heart sank. Dicky Cain would realise that I had lied to him, and retribution would be swift and sure. We filed into the classroom at one o'clock as usual, but nothing happened. The incident was not even mentioned. Perhaps he intended to keep me back at four o'clock and give me six of the best then? To my surprise, nothing was said. By the next day, I was positively hoping to be caned to get the matter done with. But again, no. In fact, the incident was never ever mentioned. Dicky knew far too much about applied psychology for such a simple solution as that. Instead, the next time someone was to go on an errand, he selected someone other than me for the first time. I was devastated. Never again did he ask me to go, and I felt awful. To this day, I can recall the remorse that I felt because of my split loyalties. I had betrayed his trust, and he knew that I knew how much I had fallen in his esteem.

There were various little rituals in the school that I wished that I could be part of. For example, some pupils came from Baldwin and Abbeylands by school bus and, at a quarter to four, they were allowed to leave the class to catch the bus home. The idea of being officially allowed to leave the class fifteen minutes early each day appealed to me very much, but unfortunately I never qualified. At dinnertime, the out-of-town boys were allowed to boil a kettle of water to make cocoa. They each had a little container, such as an Oxo tin, in which they had a mixture of cocoa and sugar. They were allowed to have a drink and eat their sandwiches inside the school building, which was something of a privilege, as the rest of us were obliged to remain outside, no matter how cold or wet the weather was.

Another group that I envied were those who received free footwear. Up to about 1935 they all, both boys and girls, received clogs. After this time, they were given boots. We all, as a routine, had our boots or shoes inspected by the teacher, and we would be told off if they did not come up to expectations. However, the pupils who had the free issue came in for special attention. If the teacher felt that they were unacceptably dirty (and they did not have to be very bad to qualify) the pupil would be sent home to get them cleaned. But either way, clogs or boots, I felt that they were lucky to get them, as I was obliged to wear shoes bought from Marks and Spencer's, whose soles were made out of compressed cardboard. They cost five shillings (25p) a pair and, although they looked good, particularly when new, they soon sprung leaks. I then had to fit cardboard inner soles until such time that the uppers gave up the ghost completely. Five shillings was a lot of money to spend on a pair of shoes, as my father probably earned less that two pounds a week if he was in full-time work, and often he was only on half- time. One can only wonder how small the family income had to be before children qualified for the free issue. In my case, the shoes represented something of a no-win situation, in that no matter how carefully they were looked after, they all too soon needed replacing. Therefore, the time would arrive when my mother had to juggle the cash flow situation to budget for another pair. It must have been a struggle for her, although I was not particularly aware of it, for when the next pair was required she would do her magic and they would appear. Remarkably, she never complained about me playing football in the street, or, for that matter, any other game that would hasten the end of the shoes.

Another ritual was free school dinner. Each morning various children (usually those who had the free boots) were given tickets to take to Noble's Hall, which stood on the tar patch at the corner of Tynwald Street and Westmoreland Road. There, they exchanged the ticket for a free, hot meal. I thought that they received this munificence because they had been lucky in some sort of raffle of which I was unaware. There was never any feeling that these children were inferior or disadvantaged - just a slight feeling of envy on the part of the rest of us that they kept winning the raffle. It was the same with school milk. Every day the lucky ones (i.e., boots and dinners) received a third of a pint of milk free, whilst the rest of us either bought it for a halfpenny (1/4p) or did without. Although I did not realise it at the time, whether or not I had money to buy the milk was a measure of how good or bad the cash situation was at home. The classrooms had central heating, but the furnace was fed so sparingly that the pipes were barely warm. In the winter the milk was partly frozen, although it had rested on the radiator for over an hour. I remember that the classrooms were sometimes very cold.

Strangely enough, I never made the connection between the free milk, boots and dinners for some children and the visit to the school once a year by the 'Nit Nurse'. When she came, we lined up in single file to be examined. We had our height measured, were weighed, she looked at our eyes and carried out a few other checks that I can no longer remember. However, the one thing that I recollect clearly is that she examined our hair closely. I do not know why she bothered, because I am sure that almost all of us must have had nits. How could it be otherwise, in spite of the best efforts of our parents? Every Sunday morning I had to kneel in front of my mother whilst she scraped away at my hair with a fine-tooth comb. However, it was to no avail, as at school we each wore a cap, and a favourite pastime was wearing one belonging to somebody else, anyone else. So as fast as the battle of the nits was won, we would promptly re-infect our hair.

Although the visit of the 'Nit Nurse' did not bother us unduly that of the dentist most certainly did. He was known as Cod-eyes because of his thick-lens glasses. I do not think that any of us ever knew what his real name was. We all tried to think of ways of missing the dental inspection, but no one succeeded as far as I know. You may think we could have stayed away from school that day, but we never had any inkling that he was coming until it was too late. Cod-eyes had a complete set of cards, one for every boy in the school. Whilst he examined your teeth he would call out mystic numbers to his assistant, who literally 'marked your card'. A few long days later the teacher handed out pink cards, which confirmed that you required dental treatment. Groans could be heard from all over the classroom as we learned what a sorry state our teeth were in. Extractions were bad enough, but fillings were even worse. After all, we knew from an early age what a visit to the dentist involved.

The dental surgery and the School Clinic were in the same building, situated on the opposite side of the road to the school in Tynwald Street, and about half way towards Westmoreland Road. The clinic was on the ground floor, whilst the surgery was on the first floor. Everywhere was spotlessly clean and the linoleum on the floor was highly polished, a tribute to Mrs. Turner who lived 'over the shop'. She had two daughters, Monica and Audrey, both of whom went to the Girls High School. Monica was about my age. She was lovely, and I had something of a crush on her, although I never told her. Even so, I hated the place where she lived.

When the time came to report to the dentist for treatment, you climbed the stairs to the front room on the first floor. There you waited for the summons to the surgery proper. The room was large and bare, except for a large, dark-coloured mattress on the floor and a few books that you could pretend to read whilst awaiting your turn. Sometimes shrieks and howls came from the surgery, but they were clearly of no avail, because the unfortunate boy never appeared before the job was done. I found this sad, as it meant that particular ploy was a non-starter.

When it was my turn to enter the 'torture chamber' I always tried to do it with as much dignity and nonchalance as I could muster - probably very little, in fact. Cod-eyes had a card in his hand as he gestured you to sit in the chair. You were not consulted in any way about what was going to happen to you. You just kept your mouth open as he poked about, your head pushed firmly against the headrest. I have two overriding impressions of being in that position. One is of those great big eyes peering into me - sometimes I wondered just how far into my body he could see. The other is my morbid fascination with the drilling machine. It was operated by a foot pedal, which drove a large metal wheel, about eighteen inches in diameter. An endless cord joined this wheel to a smaller one, located about three feet above it. This smaller wheel was geared to the drill, so the speed at which the drill turned was governed directly by the speed at which Cod-eyes pedalled. This fearful machine stood immobile but ever threatening as he decided which teeth he would work on first.

If his hand came into view holding a syringe, I would heave a slight (very slight) sigh of relief, as it meant that he was going to pull one or more teeth out. This was bad enough, but not nearly as frightening as him reaching for the drill. Fillings were carried out without an injection and, as the machine was pedalled quite casually, the drill did not rotate very fast, so filling a tooth was a slow and painful process. On the other hand, if you were to have an extraction, you were given an injection of cocaine. The syringes and needles were very large compared to those used today, so an injection was quite painful. After the injection, you were sent back to the waiting room for about ten minutes while your mouth 'froze'. Meanwhile, some other unfortunate who had already been 'frozen', would be called back to the surgery. More wailing and howling could often be heard, which did little to reassure the person in the waiting room.

I do not know to this day what Cod-eyes real name was. He must have had the most unrewarding job in the whole of the Island. In retrospect we owe him a debt of gratitude, for he seemed to work most conscientiously at salvaging what he could of our neglected teeth. I do not suppose many children cleaned their teeth at that time, as toothpaste was considered something of a luxury. For a course of treatment by Cod-eyes, my parents had to pay sixpence (3p), and this they always paid. However, if they wished they could opt to have the treatment carried out privately. The cost of this would have been prohibitive, so it was a non-starter for me. Nevertheless, this did not stop me begging them to pay up, as I had convinced myself that private treatment would be painless.

My brother George passed through Demesne Road School a few years before me, and had been a leading light in the football team. Therefore, I was in a favoured position, so soon I, too, had been selected to play for the school team. The captain was Frank Daugherty, whose mother had a sweet shop in Allan Street. Robert Fargher was the goalkeeper, and I played on the left wing. We were not very good, as we lost more games than we won. On one particularly humiliating day, we were beaten by nine goals to nil by Rushen School. However, we usually managed to beat St. Mary's.

By way of compensation, though, we swept the board at swimming. This was mainly because Alfie Tate attended the school, and he was a superb swimmer. His father was the attendant at Noble's Baths in Victoria Street, and he, too, was very good. His children must have spent all their free time there, as they were like fish in the water. As far as I know, Alfie became the attendant after his father retired. However, to get back to the story, once a year all the elementary schools competed in the Grand Swimming Gala. Alfie entered every event that he could, and his equally talented sister, representing Tynwald Street, entered all the girls' events. Between them they won every single cup, shield and medal for which they competed. For example, Alfie could swim underwater, collect twenty plates off the bottom, and still swim up and down the length of the pool to ensure that he had not missed any, before surfacing. He really was very good. Consequently, the table that stood on the dais in the school hall was crowded to overflowing with trophies.

Very occasionally, we were taken to the pictures (the cinema) from school. For example, the Grand Theatre stood next to Noble's Baths. As the name suggests, it had started life as a theatre, but latterly was also used as a cinema. I remember seeing 'Journey's End' and 'The Garden of Allah' there. However, the owners, the Palace and Derby Castle Company, decided that it needed a face-lift. It resurfaced as the Regal Cinema. The very first film shown was 'Clive of India', and a special matinee was laid on for the schoolchildren. It cost three pence, but was worth it, as there was lots of fighting and, of course, the British won. The noise must have been deafening, what with the battle scenes and all of us bawling encouragement to our side.

Another film which I remember seeing there was 'Sixty Glorious Years', about the reign of Queen Victoria. We all had high hopes of lots of battle scenes, so we were quite disappointed to find that the story revolved around the life of the Queen herself. As it happens, I saw this film recently on the television, and I thought it was very good. Although we boys did not think much of it at the time, I expect the girls liked it.

The top class at Demesne Road was Form IV. The teacher was Mr. Clucas, whom we affectionately called Clutch, because he had a deformity to one foot. We held him in very high regard. He was quietly spoken, but had complete authority in the classroom. He rarely needed to cane anyone, unlike Mr. Moyer who was in charge of the woodwork class at Raphael Road. He made wrongdoers bend over and touch their toes, and then lightly tapped your bottom with his cane whilst he gave a little sermon about your behaviour, before delivering the real strokes. They could not have been hard really, as none of us ever had any marks afterwards, although we all firmly believed that we were being punished piteously. Even so, we liked woodwork, although in my case I was hopeless at it. The main attraction was that Mr. Moyer would leave the class for several minutes from time to time. As soon as this happened we would stampede to the wooden wall which separated us from the gymnasium. Over the years many holes had been drilled through the wall (after all, the tools were immediately to hand) and we would scramble to get a good view of the girls doing PT (physical training) in their navy-blue knickers and white vests. This forbidden sight fascinated me.

As for the woodwork itself, I recall making a money box whose dovetail joints were so poor that the box only held together because of the prodigious amount of fish glue that I poured into it. I then graduated to making a coffee table. This was never completed, as the legs were all different lengths, and I could never get them all to match. My skill at woodworking was akin to that of my knitting.

By way of compensation, though, I did well at essay writing. In fact, in my last year at school in 1939, I won the Manx Temperance Federation Essay Competition, which was open to all the elementary schools on the Island. For this, the school was given the custody of a

The obverse and reverse of the Manx Temperance Federation Essay Competition medal, which I won in 1939. The actual size is 1½ x 1 inch.

large shield for a year, and I received a silver medal, the sort of thing that was worn on a watch chain in those days. I still have it. In addition, in that same year, I won the North West of England Lifeboat Essay Competition. For this I was presented with a beautiful illuminated certificate and a book about the lifeboat service called Launch.

I left school after my birthday in June 1939. The headmaster, Mr. Christian (Jacko), kindly gave me a glowing testimonial, which I still treasure. Certainly, my schooldays were very happy. All the teachers were excellent. They did not pander to the pupils in any way, and they always addressed you by your surname. You, in your turn, always addressed them as Sir or Miss. If you passed a teacher outside the school premises you were obliged to say, "Good evening, Sir" or other appropriate greeting. We saw nothing strange in this, as we all had a genuine respect for them. All of them were firm but fair in all of their dealings with us, and I suspect deep down they quite liked us. A few years after leaving school I met Dicky Cain in Strand Street when I was home on leave. I was a flight sergeant in the RAF, but he still referred to me as 'Gill' and I to him as 'Sir'. Old habits die hard, I guess. As for the canings that we got from time to time, we never harboured any grudge then or later. We knew the offences for which we would be caned, so it came as no surprise when it happened. Usually we were caned on the hand, and would dash back to our desk and firmly clasp the cold, cast-iron legs to ease the pain. Rarely did anyone cry, so it could not have been that bad.

At every school, including those for infants, the desks were two-seater, one-piece affairs. The cast iron frame had a wooden tip-up lid, which covered a small container for books. When closed, the sloping lid formed a comfortable writing surface. There was an ink well for each pupil, and the ink was made from powder mixed with water. It was poor quality stuff, and only by taking great care could you prevent getting ink blots on your work. Every blot had an accusing red ring put around it by the teacher, as did every single spelling mistake and wrong arithmetic answer. By the age of eight, everyone in the class could recite the tables up to twelve times.

All the desks faced forward, and each time that we filed into the class we would stand silently by our desk until instructed to sit down. Talking was not allowed, unless answering a question put by the teacher. This might make it seem like a very oppressive regime, but it was not so. We would whisper to each other or write notes. Some of the boys whiled away the time by catching flies (not a difficult thing to do in those days), pulling their wings off and popping them into the ink well to see how long they could survive. Some of the inkwells had so many flies in them that the ink was quite 'gooey'. Another favourite pastime was firing small paper pellets from an elastic band at other pupils. If you were caught, the teacher would give you the cane or, at the very least, a good telling-off. If he was not sure who the culprit was, he would never make the mistake of asking the class who had done it, as he knew full well that no one would 'sleech'.

The toilets were outside, in a corner of the playground, and consisted of one flush toilet per class, and a communal urinal. The toilets were all kept locked, and to get in you had to ask your teacher for the key. The urinal ran the length of the block, and was nothing more than the inner side of the outside wall. It was painted with bitumastic paint to a height of about three feet. During playtime, there would always be a line of boys standing there, each trying to pee higher than the others. Some even reached the top of the wall.

Alongside the toilets was a shelter of sorts. It was a small affair, and consisted of a roof, supported at the front by metal posts and at the rear by the schoolyard wall. Against the wall were the racks for the use of those pupils fortunate enough to have a bicycle. They were never immobilised in any way, as no one would dream of interfering with them. Even the pumps were left in place. Theft and vandalism were practically unknown either in or out of school.

Similarly, fighting was very rare. Usually fights consisted of little more than two boys staring fiercely at each other, each threatening to kill his opponent, but this was as far as it ever got. I did not have a real dispute the whole time that I was at school, and I never saw anyone else fighting. One day Dicky Cain held a poll of the class to see who was the most popular boy. To my surprise, it turned out to be me.

The classrooms were poorly furnished. Apart from the desks for the pupils, there was a more elaborate one for the teacher, one or two cupboards and a large, linen map of the World, which hung on the wall. This was most reassuring to me, for there, prominently coloured in pink, were all the countries of the British Empire, the one on which the sun never set. We did not have patriotism instilled into us, because there was no need, as we were intensely patriotic, anyway. Children today can not, perhaps, appreciate the pride and comfort that we got from looking at the map. We were certain that the Empire would last forever. How could we know that in a few short years it would be gone? Not only that, but soon even some of our own people would decry its very existence. During the morning assembly, we always sang a hymn, and one that I liked very much was sung to the tune of Harvest Home, and went:

> *Where the flag of Britain flies,*
> *Over land beyond the seas,*
> *Under dark or smiling skies,*
> *In the warm or wintry breeze...*

We sang these patriotic songs without a trace of irony, as the sentiment seemed perfectly natural and reasonable.

Occasionally, as a special treat, we were allowed to listen to one of the excellent BBC Schools wireless broadcasts. One in particular that I remember was about Imperial Airways. On another occasion, we were allowed to listen to the King Edward VIII abdication broadcast. For this, the whole school was assembled in the hall, and we sat on the floor. As the speech rambled on, we became increasingly bored. We had been told that this was a very important occasion in our history, but it seemed unimportant to us personally. Had we known that Edward was a secret Nazi sympathiser we would probably have booed him. Incidentally, the King Edward Pier in Douglas is, I believe, the only structure in the British Isles to have his name.

I was fourteen in June 1939, so shortly afterwards I left school. The class examinations were in full swing, and I was heading comfortably for the top-of-the-class position again, but I was unable to complete the examination. It was common for children to leave school as soon as possible, as parents were anxious to get them out to work to earn a bit of money for the family budget. So it was with me. That wonderful, happy and carefree part of my life was over. It had been disciplined but fair, ordered but enjoyable, and what is more, we had managed to learn quite a bit meanwhile. Every boy was passable, although, obviously, some were better than others. I did not know a single child who was illiterate or even semi-literate. It was the same with arithmetic. Even pupils at the bottom of the class could recite the tables and carry out at least the basic arithmetic operations of multiplication, division and so on. Certainly for me, and, I think, most of my contemporaries, schooldays were some of the happiest days of our lives.

CHAPTER THREE

TWENTY-EIGHT HILLSIDE AVENUE

Home sweet home

I was lucky during the depression years of the 20's and 30's. Our house was always warm and I never went hungry, because my father continued to work right through the period, at the Isle of Man Steam Packet Company. Granted, for some of the time he worked only in the afternoons, (i.e., he was on half time), but that was a whole lot better than being unemployed, which was the lot of so many others. We always had a fire in the grate and food in the house, although sometimes it did not amount to much. For example, tea would sometimes consist only of a couple of rounds of thick, toasted bread with butter, but that was most enjoyable.

I used to put so many spoonfuls of sugar in my tea that some of it was always left in the bottom of the cup. I will never know why my mother allowed it, as my father had been diabetic for as long as I could remember. As insulin was not available as a treatment for diabetes until after 1926, my father must have been one of the first people on the Island to use it. Prior to the discovery of insulin, of course, sufferers of the disease would have died. Besides putting a crazy amount of sugar in my tea, I, in common with most of the other children, had a liking for most sweet things. For example, I liked to eat bread and butter, on which was spread a thick layer of condensed milk and then a further layer of sugar. It makes me feel ill now just to think of it. Condensed milk was bought in tins, and consisted of concentrated milk mixed with an abundance of sugar, so it was a very sweet, thick, sickly mixture. I thought it was delicious at the time. No wonder that I am now slightly diabetic.

Some of my earliest memories are of the pictures that hung on the walls. At that time, all the rooms had a wooden picture rail from which the pictures were hung. The rail was about twelve inches down from the ceiling. In the downstairs back room, there hung a large picture of my father in his naval uniform. The name on the cap tally was HMS Peel Castle. It seems that he joined the Royal Navy in World War 1, but was later invalided out. He then promptly joined the army, and saw service in the Middle East and in India. I remember him telling me about the time that he was in Turkey. The Turks were advancing swiftly, and his company had to retreat to the other side of a river. As he was a good swimmer, my father stayed behind to help the poor swimmers across. However, he was surprised to find that they could cross faster than he could. He would roar with laughter as he said, "Johnny Turk made them learn to swim quickly."

Another picture that I liked hung in the living room. It was large, and showed a poorly dressed lady in a long dress. She was gently rocking a cradle whilst looking lovingly at the baby. The room was poorly furnished and illuminated only by the open fire. The caption read, 'Where your heart lies, there lies your treasure

Dad wearing his WW1 medals. The photograph was probably taken on Empire Day (May 24th), c 1933, as he always attended the parade through the town.

also.' I used to search that picture inch by inch to find the treasure, but I never found it.

In my bedroom, the picture was called 'The Angelus.' It showed two peasants standing by a wheelbarrow in a ploughed field. Their heads were bent in prayer, and each had clasped hands. I did not think much of it.

We did not have any, but at that time many people had lovely reproductions of such beautiful paintings as 'When Did You Last See Your father?'; 'The Boyhood of Raleigh'; 'The Laughing Cavalier' and, in my opinion, the nicest of them all, 'Mother and Son'. This was a picture of a mare standing lovingly near her foal. All of these pictures were obtained from cigarette companies. Each packet of twenty cigarettes contained two cards, each card a part of one of the pictures. When you had collected the fifty different cards that made up the completed picture, you could send them off, and in return received a lovely reproduction, all ready for framing and hanging. These delightful pictures brightened up many living rooms. I used to try to get my father to change to smoking the appropriate brand (Player's, I think) so that we could have one of them. However, he insisted on keeping to his favourite brands, Kensitas and Black Cat. Their cards were also very nice. For example, one series of cards had embroidered flowers. Another set showed pictures of famous footballers, printed on silk. I also recall a set of Flags of the Nations, again printed on silk. Many of the cards were educational, covering such topics as road safety; first aid; cricketers; footballers; rules of the game (for football, cricket, hockey and so on.) plus many more. Then there were the more general favourites, such as film and wireless stars - anything and everything that would attract us children, for it was us, of course, that they were aimed at. I, like all the children, collected the cards avidly, as they were the universal currency. Almost anything could be obtained with sufficient cards of the right 'sets'.

As far back as I can remember, a nightly ritual was having my chest rubbed with goose grease. I would undress down to my 'coms' (combinations) in front of the fire, and my mother would rub the stuff on me. It was such a routine, that I never got around to asking what it was supposed to do. To this day, I have no idea. In addition, I had a small gauze bag containing a block of camphor hung around my neck. The smell was nice, but again I have no idea what purpose it was supposed to serve. My brother George would pull faces at me whilst this was going on, to make me laugh. I must have given off quite a smell.

Another daily ritual was to swallow a spoonful of cod-liver oil (which I detested) followed by a spoonful of malt (which was delicious). The malt was in a square, brown bottle, and was bought in Boots. I expect all of the things that my mother rubbed and hung on me, as well as the stuff she poured down my throat were designed to make me fit and healthy, although to me, it was all a boring routine. If I fell and cut my hands or knees, I would pray that the bleeding would stop before I went into the house. Otherwise, out came the dreaded large, green, poison bottle, containing iodine. It was applied liberally to the cut, and stung like mad. I expect the theory was that if it did not sting it was not doing any good. On the other hand, if I only had a graze, then I merely had to rub nice-smelling and painless Germoline ointment on the affected part. Germoline is still obtainable today.

My father worked for many years as a sceneshifter at the Palace Coliseum. The shows put on there were, it seems, top class - the equal of any London production. My father studied the acts and developed an extensive repertoire of songs. He knew the words of all the Gilbert and Sullivan songs, those of Al Jolson, the comedy songs and the war songs. One that I used to get him to perform regularly went:

When father papered the parlour

You couldn't see Pa for paste.

Dabbing it here, dabbing it there,

Paste and paper everywhere.

Ma was stuck to the ceiling,

The kids were stuck to the floor.

You've never seen a blinking family

So stuck up before.

Another favourite that I never tired of hearing went:

She told me her age was five and twenty

Cash in the bank, she said she'd plenty.

I was a man believed it all

I was an M. U. G.

At Trinity Church, I met my doom.

Now I live in a top back room,

Up to my eyes in debt for rent

And that's what she's done for me.

He would perform all the actions to accompany the words, obviously copied very well from the stage performances. Besides being a wonderful entertainer, he was a kind and gentle man. I loved him very much.

He never hit me, but that was because I was always too quick for him. If I did something wrong, my mother would say, "See to him, Evan". At that he would jump up from his chair with a great flourish and try to catch me. But I would dash around the living room table, out of the door, up the stairs and lock myself in the toilet before he could grab me. I would often sit there and wonder why such an intelligent man always followed me around the table when he could cut me off so easily. It was years later, when I smacked one of my children in his presence that he said disapprovingly; "I never needed to do that to you." The reprimand in his voice was unmistakable, and suddenly I realised why I had always won the race around the table.

George was five years older than I was, so he organised many of the activities in the house, usually when our parents were out. Once he decided to make some toffee and another time he made bonnag. These things were barely edible, but that never put him off. He was also the leader of the Midnight Prowlers. This was a secret gang, from which I was excluded because I was too young. The gang members included boys of his age, such as Sid Shimmin and Oliver McGrath. They held regular meetings, probably to devise passwords, secret signs and so on. However, the 'Prowlers never got beyond this stage.

Another time he organised a ducking apple party. There were about five of us present, including Betty Cooile. He put water and apples in the bath, and we all started playing. I was the youngest person present, so I was also the smallest. Thus, I was obliged to stand on tiptoe to reach the apples, so I suppose it was inevitable that soon I would be in the water with them. I was undressed in front of the living room fire and dried off, whilst Betty demurely averted her gaze.

The Mona, high and dry on Connister Rocks, July 1930.
(Courtesy Manx National Heritage)

Children came and went from most of the houses as a matter of course. Our parents did not mind, as no deliberate damage was ever done. In our living room, there was a large glass container of wine, probably blackberry. George would hand out drinks to all present, with the result that the level of the wine was seriously diminished. Accordingly, he would return it to its original level by adding water. I could not believe that our parents would fail to notice that the wine was becoming anaemic. However, if they did, they did not say anything about it.

Of all the children who visited our house, the favourite with my parents and with me, was Betty Cooile. She was the daughter that they never had, and she could do no wrong in their eyes. She was a smart, good looking and intelligent girl. She and I were playmates from way back when and had many wonderful times together. We never quarrelled or fell out over anything.

In 1930, one of the Steam Packet ships, the Mona, ran aground on the rocks alongside the Tower of Refuge. It was quite a large ship, and at low tide, it was high and dry. My mother took me to join the hundreds of other sightseers who stood on the promenade to witness the extraordinary spectacle.

When I was very young, I had two comics each week, the Larks and the Funny Wonder. Later I deserted Larks and got Chips in its place. In all the picture stories, there was no blurring of the good and bad people. For example, thieves always wore a striped jersey, carried a bag marked SWAG, wore a black mask and were always caught. So, although the stories were humorous, they were also morality tales. From the comics I graduated to the adventure stories in such weekly publications as the Wizard, Rover, Hotspur, Champion and the Adventure. I only bought one, the others being obtained by swapping. They only cost two pence (1p), so were excellent value, as each contained about five stories. The English was very good, and there was always a lot of action and adventure.

The comics only cost a halfpenny (1/4p).

When I was about twelve I changed to reading Boy's Cinema. This also was a weekly publication like the Hotspur and the others, and about the same size. But now all the stories were the plots of adventure films currently being shown at the cinemas. Again, the writing was excellent, and the stories were always about adventures where virtue and heroism triumphed. Although females were allowed to intrude in a minor role, there was never any hint of sex or passion. The next progression in my reading matter was to the Sexton Blake stories. Sexton Blake was a detective who, with the help of his young assistant (with whom we all identified), could solve a baffling mystery every week. These stories were much longer than those previously, so throughout my schooldays my parents kept me supplied with lots of thoroughly enjoyable and good quality reading matter. They also bought many delightful hardback books, such as The Wonderful Story of the Sea; the World's Greatest Paintings; Wonders of the World; the Waverly Books of Knowledge, and many more. I loved reading.

One day, just before Christmas, I was walking along Strand Street with sixpence in my pocket. I would be about eight at the time and I had so much money because people had been giving me early Christmas presents. Anyway, I was determined to buy my mother a present with it, so I was heading for Woolworth's. As nothing in the whole store cost more than sixpence, I had the whole place to choose from. I settled for a colourful pot bear holding a cricket bat. He was standing on a pottery base, and behind him was a hollow container. I did not know what it was for, but bought the ornament because it was so colourful. In fact, it was intended for holding spills. Spills are rolled-up pieces of paper, used for lighting cigarettes from the fire. I dashed home with my valuable present, rushed into the house and proudly presented the brown paper parcel to my mother. It was completely unexpected, and she was very pleased with it. I recall asking her what it was for, and she told me. She had tears running

Mother and Dad, taken about 1935, in the back garden of 28 Hillside Avenue.

down her cheeks, and I asked her what was wrong, but she just held me close to her. That spill holder remained on the mantle piece until my parents died.

Every summer the house was full of visitors. I do not know how they were all packed in, as it was only a three-bedroom house. I was happy, as I had a comfortable bed on the floor of the pantry. This suited me fine, as the chocolate biscuits were stored there, so I had many a private feast. I do not recall much about the visitors, as I had very little dealings with them. However, I was expected to help with various jobs such as shelling peas or operating the clothes washing machine. The machine was a hand operated affair, and my job was to move the agitator handle back and forth a hundred and fifty times for each wash. I always did the correct number, but the speed of the agitation depended upon my mood. The machine was advertised as The Housewife's Darling. My father bought it brand new, and my mother was overjoyed with it. A few years ago, I visited a small domestic museum in Shaftesbury, and there, to my amazement, was the same Housewife's Darling that I had lavished so much energy on as a boy. It seems incredible that something I can remember so clearly is now a museum piece. I suppose this might be a definition of being old.

We also had a Ewbank carpet sweeper. It was a sturdy, hand operated machine which, when pushed, caused two brushes to rotate. Similar machines are still available today, but now they are made of plastic, so are lighter and easier to use. The carpets, of course, were only small. When they required more cleaning than the Ewbank could provide, the carpets were draped over the clothes line and given a good thumping, using a specially shaped beater made of strong cane. Wall to wall carpeting was unheard-of in working class houses. The usual floor layout was to have the floorboards visible for about a foot from each wall, usually painted a dark colour or stained with permanganate of potash. Then there was a square of cheap linoleum covering the main part of the floor with, in strategic locations such as in front of the fireplace, a rag or wool mat. This was also the basic pattern for the bedrooms. The stairs were usually covered with a strip of linoleum about eighteen inches wide and held in position with brass stair rods.

The furniture was usually cheap, and often was obtained from catalogue clubs. The one my mother was in was called the Sartorial Club. Thus, we had in the living room, beside the mats, a cheap three-piece suite, a dining table with four chairs and a sideboard. The coal fire was contained in a steel and cast iron kitchen range. This fire heated the room, the water and the oven. Sometimes, if the fire had been going well and no water had been run off for a while, there would be a thunderous banging when the water in the back-boiler boiled. There would be a rush to run some hot water off to stop the awful noise. The banging dislodged scale and rust from the system, so we always filled the kettle with cold water. Even today, I can not break the habit.

In those days, kettles did not have an automatic cut-out. Consequently, when the water boiled steam issued from the spout in great quantities. If the kettle was left boiling, the room filled with water vapour, and rivulets of condensation ran down the walls and windows. This is why whistling kettles were introduced. These had a whistle built into the filling-hole lid. When the kettle boiled the steam generated was discharged through the whistle, and so gave off a piercing shriek. If, though, you were slow to respond, the force of the steam was sufficient to push the whistle off, so you were back to square one. Even the electric kettles did not have a cut-out fitted.

The Hillside Avenue houses were new, so we had all the modern conveniences, such as electric lighting; an indoors flush toilet, a bath and a gas supply for cooking. There was also a garden at the front and the rear. All-in-all, we were very fortunate. Many houses in Douglas had gas lighting until after World War Two.

Corporation houses such as ours had the water rate and the electricity charge included with the rent. However, the amount of electricity that you could use at any one time was very little. Of course, there was only lighting to consider, as there were no power points installed. Even so, if more than about three moderate size bulbs were lit at the same time, then all the lights would flicker rapidly on and off until the permitted loading was restored. The flickering was initiated by a 'load limiter', usually just called the limiter. It was located next to the meter. Consequently, there was a powerful incentive to use very low-wattage lamps. Thus, the bedrooms would have, say, 15 watt bulbs, landings and toilet 5 watt neon lamps and the living room a 40 or even 60 watt lamp. We must have groped about like troglodytes in the semi-darkness. By 1938, many of the tenants had opted to have pre-payment meters, so the limiter was removed. It, therefore, gradually became less common for us, whilst playing in the street, to see the lights flickering in someone's house. However, some remained until about 1938. The pre-payment meters were always called slot meters. In the case of gas, it required a penny in the slot. As a back up, in case pennies were not available when required, we had a strategic reserve of foreign coins, which would do the job. There was no intention to defraud, as, when the man came to empty the meter, he would give my mother the refund less the value of these coins. He also returned the coins so that they could be put back into the reserve. I think the meter man was Mr. Lord, or perhaps he was the rent man.

We had a number of lodgers staying with us over the years. One was Wilf Wickman. He was a superb painter and decorator, and he painted the woodwork in the front room to a professional standard. He was a quiet but charming chap. My favourite lodger, though, was Percy Broad. He was about eighteen, devil-may-care and usually short of money. He was good looking and had red hair, so he was very popular with the young girl visitors who stayed with us. In fact, he ended up marrying one of them; a charming girl called Joan Blease. Percy joined the army in 1937, and that was the last that I saw of him.

One thing that I will always remember him for is that he took me to see the one and only wrestling promotion that I have ever seen. It was held at the Palais de Danse, and I became a fan of the Blue Mask. I thoroughly enjoyed that evening.

Shortly after Percy left, his brother George came to stay for a short while. This short stay lasted for many years, until long after the war. George Broad was a professional pianist, and he had a studio over Blakemore's music shop in Victoria Street. In the summer, he played in the orchestra at the Palace Coliseum. He was a talented musician, and later gained his L.R.A.M. He gave several concerts in the Gaiety Theatre, and often accompanied Dan Minay, a well-known local singer, and various others.

Jumping ahead, he served in the RAF at Jurby during the war, as a ground wireless operator. He played the piano in the station's concert party. Once, the top star in the country, George Formby, gave a guest appearance there. As with all the best show business stories, his piano accompanist could not play, as his wife was ill. Therefore, George Broad stood in for him. He did such a good job, that George Formby asked him to tour with him. This would be until his own man could rejoin him. I would have thought that most people would have jumped at such a chance, but he turned the offer down. He could do no wrong in my mother's eyes, as he would play any music that she requested. I was less impressed and, in fact, we kept our distance from each other. It was the 1950's when he left my parent's house.

It was very often cold in the house in the winter. The living room had heating from the coal fire and, if the gas stove was in use, the kitchen was warm. The rest of the house was like an icebox. The bed sheets were made of flannelette because it felt warmer, but even so, when I climbed into bed I would curl up into a ball to keep as warm as possible. Of course, in the morning, it felt wonderfully warm, and it was a shame to have to get up. George and I shared the bed for some years, but as he was five years older, he was allowed to

The RAF Jurby 'Aeronautics' dance band. George Broad is at the piano; Harold Moorhouse is on drums. Station Warrant Officer Cyril Ratcliffe is standing at the rear; and the conductor is Jack Hart who, before the war, led a successful London band.

stay up much later than me, so I was usually fast asleep by the time he came to bed. If it was particularly cold, I would sleep with my woollen school stockings on. The trouble with that, though, was that in the morning it took ages to pull all the little balls of flannelette out of the wool.

Until the early 1930's, the main entertainment that we had in the house was a wind-up Decca gramophone. Records could be bought in Woolworth's for three pence or six pence, so we had a reasonable collection, usually of the 'Oh, For the Wings of a Dove' type. One of my favourite records had 'In A Monastery Garden' on one side and 'In A Persian Market' on the other. Another favourite was 'Shepherd of the Hills'. However, one day in about 1932 the gramophone was forgotten, as Ernie, my eldest brother, brought us a wireless set. It was home made, and the pieces were mounted on a plywood base. The front panel was a piece of ebonite, and the various controls were mounted on it. The main control was the tuner, a circular affair with mysterious numbers on the dial. The aerial was a length of copper wire slung between the eaves of our house and those of Mrs. Cooile's opposite. As more and more people acquired wireless sets, the avenue sprouted a canopy of aerials. They were not very popular with us children, as our kites became entangled with them and could not be retrieved. But the wireless set itself was magic. I could not understand where the sound was coming from. I used to stare at the exposed components and wonder how those inanimate valves and pieces of wire could produce the speech and music that came from the loud speaker.

That early set, though, had to be treated reverentially, for it suffered from 'oscillations'. As you turned the tuning dial, the most hideous noises were produced. This was due to the technical affliction known as oscillation. It was so bad that my mother gave strict instructions that we must not interfere with the tuning once good reception was obtained. I ignored her, as it was so exciting to play with the tuner to find as many stations as possible, hidden away amongst the shrieks and howls. Wireless was so new that I remember Cecil Cowell, who lived in number thirty-nine, inviting several of us into his house (whilst his parents were out) to let us look at their brand new Ecko wireless set. The case was circular, and made of black Bakelite, and to me it was the last word in elegance, particularly when it was switched on and several stations were received without the dreaded oscillation. Cecil said, proudly and mysteriously, "Of course, it's a five-valve superhet." We all nodded wisely, but really, we had no more idea of what a five-valve superhet was, than did Cecil. However, what we did know was that, whatever it meant, it was a good thing to have, for all the adverts for modern wirelesses stressed the point.

Finally, in 1935, the day came when my father bought a brand new five-valve superhet wireless of our own. It was made by His Master's Voice, and the case was made of highly polished wood veneer. It was beautiful. It had long, medium and short wave reception, and the tuning dial was a rectangular piece of glass upon which the names of many stations were painted. The location of most of them was a complete mystery to me - places such as Hilversum, Luxemburg, Budapest and so on. In fact, I was not even sure where the BBC stations of Droitwich and Daventry were. In any case, it did not matter where they were. All that mattered was that the broadcasts could be received without interference. It was of particular interest to tune in to foreign stations to listen to the language. I had not heard any language other than English in my whole life, except for a few words of Manx. I would spend hours tuning in to different stations to listen to the foreigners jabbering away and wondering what they were talking about.

The world was changing rapidly in the 1930's. Not only was wireless becoming quite common, but so, also, were motor cars and aeroplanes. If we heard an aeroplane engine, we would rush out of doors to look for the aircraft. There were also giant airships, such as the Hindenburg, flying to the USA. Extensive coverage of pioneering flights was given in the papers and on the wireless. We regarded the fliers with the same sort of admiration that we had for the film stars. When Amy Johnson flew solo from England to Australia in a Gypsy Moth aeroplane, for example, a popular song was written about her exploit. The record sold for three pence in Woolworth's and was a best seller. I remember the words well:

Amy, wonderful Amy,

How can you blame me

For loving you?

Since you won the pride of every nation,

You have filled my heart with admiration.

Amy, wonderful Amy,

We're proud of the way you flew.

Believe me, Amy, you cannot blame me, Amy,

For falling in love with you.

In September 1934, a new luxury liner was to be launched at Clydebank by the Queen. It was to be the largest ship in the world, but until its launch it did not have a name - only a number, the 534. The excitement was intense throughout the land, and there was much speculation about its name. Finally the time came for the launch, and the name was revealed - the Queen Mary.

I am struck by the tremendous excitement that we felt in what was happening around us, compared to the almost cursory interest shown, say, in the astronauts in recent years. Perhaps we have become too sophisticated and blasé.

Anyway, to return to the pre-war wireless sets, our HMV model was a mains set. However, in those households with gas lighting, the wireless was operated from a 100-volt dry battery. This consisted of seventy AA type cells wired in series to give the correct voltage. The battery would last a reasonable length of time, but when the voltage could no longer be sustained it needed to be replaced. In addition, a grid bias battery was required. Like five-valve superhet, this was another term, which we used without the slightest idea of what it meant. However, we knew that you must have one. The battery operated at twelve volts, again consisting of dry cells. There were also 1.5 volt wet batteries, and these could be re-charged. The battery case was made of thick glass and was fitted with a carrying handle. It could be re-charged at garages and electrical shops, such as at Lawton's in John Street. The charging load was usually three or four carbon filament lamps, which gave off a characteristic yellow light, the reason that they were not used for straightforward lighting. The demand for such charging facilities lasted until after World War Two..

Coal was the usual fuel burnt in houses, so the chimneys became lined with soot. Of course, they should have been cleaned at regular intervals, but to most people such expense could be postponed indefinitely. The result was that it was quite common to see chimney fires. A huge cloud of thick, black smoke, soot and sparks poured from the chimney. It looked spectacular and was potentially dangerous. However, this did not disturb us children, for we knew that, with a little luck, the fire would get out of control and the fire brigade would be called. Strangely enough, I can not recall a single fire being started from a chimney fire, which must surely rank as something of a miracle.

In the summer, there were many flies about. Only people with enough money had houses that had a refrigerator, so food storage was something of a problem, hence the number of flies. Fly swatters could be bought for three pence in Woolworth's, but rolled-up newspaper did just as well. Flycatchers cost about a penny (1/2p) and consisted of a small red-coloured cardboard cylinder, inside which was a loosely rolled length of paper covered in thick glue, and with one end of the paper attached to the inside of the cylinder. The idea was that you pulled the free end of the paper until it hung in a spiral from the case. It was then suspended in the room, and any fly or bluebottle that landed on it was unable to get free. The device would be left in position for, say, two weeks, after which time it would be black with flies. Food was kept away from the flies in a meat safe, which was a roomy cupboard that had metal gauze panels on the doors.

Milk was bought daily. We usually got ours from a farmer called Stanley Moore, whose farm was just outside Douglas. He did his round in a horse-drawn milk cart, which had a large, gleaming, metal churn. You took your jug out to him and he measured the milk in certified vessels, usually a pint, half pint or a gill. Technically, a gill is a half-pint, but on the Island, it was always regarded as a quarter of a pint. Bottled milk was delivered in the green Ellersley Dairy's vans. This Manx farm was the first in the British Isles to have its entire herd tuberculin tested, so the milk was known as TT milk. For long enough I wondered what the connection was between the milk and the races.

If we ran out, I was sent to Mrs. Waterson's milk house. It was the next to the top house in Drinkwater Street, at the junction with Circular Road. Oates and Brownbill's grocery shop was two doors away. In the milk house you descended the stairs and waited at the bottom where a cowbell hung from the banister. You gave the bell a good ding-dong and waited to be served. The place was spotlessly clean and the milk was kept on a long, cool slab. You brought your own jug, and a favourite pastime of mine was, on the way home, to see how slowly I could swing the filled jug vertically, without spilling the contents. Inevitably, the day came when I lost, and emptied the milk all over me. I felt certain that my mother would give me a good hiding but, to my joy and amazement, she thought it was funny, and laughed as she sent me back to get another pint.

My brother George worked at the Onchan Co-op. grocery store, so of necessity was obliged to bicycle to and from work. As was common at that time, the bicycle had an acetylene lamp, an ingenious device that gave off a bright, white light. The lamp had a small reservoir of water, and this was allowed to drip, in a controlled manner, on to a piece of solid carbide. This caused acetylene gas to be given off, which was piped to the front of the lamp. The gas was lit at the pipe outlet and gave a very good flame. The trouble was, though, that the smell of the acetylene gas was awful, particularly if released inside the house, and George managed to do it quite often. The doors and windows had to be opened wide to get rid of the smell, no matter how cold the weather.

He worked very long hours, particularly during the summer, and often he would not get home until ten or eleven o'clock, but he always remained cheerful. One winter evening he came home and produced a large, wind-up Hornby locomotive, which he gave to me straight away. I would be nine or ten at the time and had never had such a wonderful present in all my life. It seems that one of the Co-op customers had been kind enough to give it to him. Having got the locomotive, the problem of what to get me for my birthday and Christmas presents was solved. Over the years, I amassed a long length of track, signals, various goods trucks, buffers and so on. Frequently I would lay out the track on the living room floor and play with my train set for hours, often until I was too tired to put the track away, so my long-suffering dad would do it. After some years, my mother gave this valuable and extensive kit away to a relative whom I did not even know. By that time it required a large suitcase to hold it all, mostly provided by my eldest brother, Ernie, and his charming wife, Emmy. They lived in number twenty-one Peel Road. I also received nice presents from my other brothers. One in particular that I recall was from Charles and his wife, Nellie. It was an optical kit called Construments, which enabled me to perform simple, but interesting, experiments.

Another educational kit was given to me by our next door neighbour, Mrs. Kermode. She lived in number twenty-nine, and she was a smart, striking and cheerful woman whom I liked very much. She had two children, Frank and Mary, both of whom went to the High School. Frank was a few years older than me, and his mother gave me a large chemistry set for which he had no further use. This was very kind of them.

The neighbours on the other side (number twenty-seven) were called Killey. Again, they were a charming family. Mr. Killey worked as a coal heaver. He was not a big man, but he must have been quite strong, as the work was very hard indeed. When one of the 'Ben' boats (i.e., Ben Voar, Ben Voirry, Ben Veg, Ben Ellen) docked, the holds were full of loose coal. Huge, round, wooden tubs were lowered into the hold by crane, and it was the coal-heaver's job to fill them, using a large shovel. The tubs were then craned to waiting lorries for distribution. The work continued in all weather, so it must have been uncomfortable, as well as phisically demanding work at times. The Killey's had two sons, Douglas and Marshall. Marshall was about my age and I often played in his house. Two of the things that I remember about his home are the framed certificate awarded to Mr. Killey for bravery, and a large picture of the Steam Packet ship Ellan Vannin, which hung in the living room. This ship foundered at the mouth of the River Mersey with considerable loss of life, and the name was never used again. I loved looking at that picture. Marshall's uncle drove a lorry for a firm called L. L. Corkill, and each working day he went to Mrs. Killey's for his dinner. The lorry was parked outside, and Marshall would nonchalantly climb in, start it up and drive it along Hillside Avenue, up Hillside Terrace, along Westmoreland Road and back to his house. He was a very competent driver, and we envied his skill.

My father used to eat some food that I did not like at all. For example, there was always a large dish of pickled herrings in the kitchen waiting to be cooked. The fish lay under brine, liberally dosed with spices of various colours. To me it looked and tasted awful. Another of his favourites was tripe. He would eat a large piece for his supper, after adding lots of salt, pepper and vinegar. I thought it was tasteless. There were several shops in Douglas that specialised in preparing tripe, known as tripe dressers, so it must have been popular. There was at least Makin's in Strand Street and Clague's at the bottom of Police Station Hill. Dad also liked brawn, black puddings and pigs trotters. Later, even I learned to like savoury ducks, bought from Clague's, although I never had the courage to enquire what they were made of.

From time to time, we had rabbit pie, a meal that we all enjoyed. The rabbit had to be skinned and gutted, but this was a job that Dad could do easily and expertly. However, my favourite meal was Lancashire hot pot. It was cooked in the coal-fired oven, as were most of the meals, and it was so mouth watering that I can still smell and taste it.

From when I was very young we had a collie dog called Jack, and I loved him. Each day he would wait for me coming home from school. He would sit outside number twelve and look up the hill for me, ignoring all the other children. As soon as I appeared he would race up the hill and jump up for me to put my cap in his mouth. He would then rush along the avenue with it firmly clenched in his teeth, with me chasing breathlessly behind him. He would stop at the gate for me to catch up, before dropping the cap. He was never bad tempered, snarled or attempted to bite, although I sometimes deserved it. For instance, sometimes I would sit on his back and slap him to go, or tie him between the shafts of my bogey to get him to pull it like a dogcart. But Jack was not stupid. Although he accepted the things that I did to him, he would not move. He just stood there until I got tired of the battle of wills and let him go. He could bound over the palings in front of the house with ease and, if the occasion demanded it, run

Miserable-looking me sitting on a visitor's knee, with our dog, Jack, for company, c 1931.

like the wind. However, one day it all went wrong. Whether he was getting old or whether he slipped I will never know. We were having tea, when there was a commotion at the front of the house. We went to see what the trouble was, and there, embedded on the palings, was Jack. He was in a dreadful state, as the pointed tops had pierced his body. Dad lifted him clear, and gently carried him into the house. He tended Jack for weeks, as he made a slow recovery. Doubtless Dad was getting advice from the Steam Packet's vet. Jack made a full recovery but, in 1937, he died after eating some food that had been poisoned. Perhaps it was an accident, as the food may have been intended for a rodent, but that was little consolation to me. It was the first time that I could remember feeling so sad.

Later we had a Manx cat called Greeba. Not only was she Manx, but she was born with just three legs. However, the handicap did not seem to interfere with her mobility, as she could run, jump and do all the usual things with apparent ease. Although I liked Greeba, she was never in the same league for my affection as was Jack. I expect the basic trouble was that cats can not do things, such as jumping up for one's cap.

After Jack, my father soon had another nursing job. My mother's left leg became very painful, and gradually got worse until she could no longer stand on it. She could not climb the stairs, so to get to the bedroom she was obliged to sit on her bottom and go up the stairs backwards. Of all the adversity with which she had to cope, this was the only time that I saw her cry with despair. She was convinced that she would never walk again. Every day my father bandaged her leg from calf to thigh. The bandage was soaked in a mixture of salamoniac and vinegar, and the nursing went on for months. Of course, Dad had still to go to work, do the cooking and clean the house whilst mother was ill. I am ashamed to admit that, as far as I can remember, I did nothing to help. However, mother gradually recovered the use of her leg and, although not as good as new, at least she could get around in reasonable comfort.

Then it was Dad's turn. Phlebitis developed in his right leg, and he was confined to bed for several weeks. It is a serious ailment, so it must have been very worrying for my parents, not least the fear that his wages would be stopped, or at least drastically reduced. But I recall one evening, when I was playing a game of draughts with him, he said mysteriously, "We're alright for money, you know. They're looking after me." I took this to mean that his pay, or at least part of it, was continuing during his illness, so it must have been a tremendous relief to my parents. Although he was a very active man, Dad never complained about his enforced idleness. He had a wire cage over his leg to keep the bedclothes off, and he had to keep the leg as still as possible. After some weeks he made a complete recovery and was able to return to work. Meanwhile my mother was also much better, so things began to get back to normal at number twenty-eight. It did not occur to me at the time, but it was indeed fortunate that the ailments of my mother and father did not occur simultaneously.

From the back door of the house there were a couple of steps leading down to the path, which also formed a mini yard. This is where the mangle stood, a large, cast iron affair about four feet high. Attached to the frame was a large cast iron wheel with a handle to turn the heavy wooden rollers. The pressure on the rollers could be adjusted by altering the setting of a large leaf spring, although I never knew it to be altered. The weekly ritual in most homes was to wash and dry the clothes on Monday. The next day they were ironed and aired. Everything was done by hand, usually by the lady of the house. An important part of the process was 'dollying' the clothes. For this, the clothes were put in a large, circular, ribbed dolly-tub, which stood about three feet high. It was filled with water to which a Reckitt's 'blue bag' was added. This gave the water a blue colour, and helped to make the clothes extra white. A dolly peg was a stout wooden shaft, which had three short legs at the bottom, and by rapidly lifting and lowering the peg, you caused considerable agitation of the clothes. After being washed, the clothes were passed through the

Circa 1935. I do not remember being so unsmiling, but that is how many of my photographs appeared. Notice that the suit is too big for me (to allow room for me to 'grow into it'). Also, notice the mangle in Mrs. Kermode's house, next door.

mangle. This was a skilled job, as a lady would normally do it on her own. She would lift, say, double bed sheets out of the water, fold them roughly, admit the end to the mangle and then, whilst turning the machine, retrieve them from the other side. The mangles were so big and strong that anything from double blankets down could be passed through. We used to laugh at a naughty song about how careful large women had to be when mangling, to ensure that they did not stand too close and pass themselves through.

The ironing was done with either a box iron or a flat iron. Box irons were made of metal in the shape of a hollow pointed box, about four inches high. At the back, there was a lift-up door to permit a suitably shaped block of red hot metal to be inserted. There were several such blocks, one in use and the others heating in the fire. The flat iron, on the other hand, was just one piece of metal, so it was all heated. Thus, it was necessary to wrap a cloth around the handle when using it. Electric irons could be purchased from places such as Marks and Spencer's for five shillings (25p). They were usually operated from a light socket, so Woolworth's obligingly sold adapters, which could be plugged into the lamp holder. This provided a socket for an appliance, such as an iron, plus a lamp holder. So, you had light to see what you were doing whilst you ironed.

Wednesday was window-cleaning day. The windows were of the sash-cord type, so to clean the upstairs ones it was necessary for Mum to sit on the window cill, with her back to the road. She cleaned with one hand and held on with the other. I must say that, from my recollection, leisure was in short supply for the homemakers in those days. Every day seems to have been accounted for, and usually involved a lot of hard work. I expect cleaning the windows was regarded as nothing of a job. The work was the same for everyone, so my mother was only doing the same as everyone else. That was how it had been for ages, and that was how it would remain for the foreseeable future. It was the early post war years before any real improvement took place, with appliances such as automatic washing machines and electrically operated wringers at last becoming available at a reasonable price.

I, like most children, I suppose, loved to rummage through the dressing table drawers in my mother's bedroom. I was particularly fascinated by the items of attire that I was not permitted to see when worn, such as corsets. These were large garments, usually made of pink material. There were several panels, which were reinforced by lengths of wire, and the whole contraption was laced tightly in position when worn. It must have been a formidable piece of body armour. One item, for which I could not think of a use, consisted merely of about two feet of soft, elasticised material, the thickness of string. It had a small loop at one end, and a small button at the other, sized to fit easily into the loop. Clearly, it was intended to fit round one's waist, but for what purpose? It was a wonderful world of childish curiosity and innocence we inhabited in those far-off days.

At the time of the coronation of George VI, May 12th 1937, the Douglas Corporation announced a competition to find the best decorated council house for the occasion. My parents devoted a lot of time, effort and an abundance of red, white and blue paper to make twenty-eight quite special. Their energy was deemed worthwhile when they were awarded the first prize.

When I was very young, we would usually have a bonfire in the back garden to which anyone could come. Besides the usual bangers, sparklers, flip-flops and catherine wheels, my dad usually managed to get a box of time-expired distress flares, which gave off brilliant coloured flames and lasted for a long time, so we always had a grand time. Later, though, the general rule was for the avenue children to have a communal fire, usually at the bottom end of the lane behind the avenue. However, ours could never compete with the one held on the tar patch in Westmoreland Road. This usually necessitated a fire engine standing-by in case it got out of control, because Ashton's Ford Depot, a large garage, was just across the road. Another excellent fire was that on the shore, and this one had

28 Hillside Avenue all dressed up for the Coronation of King George VI. My parents won first prize for their effort. Mrs. Killey's house is on the left.

the advantage that, when it was finished, one simply waited for the tide to remove the debris.

All through my childhood, a nightly ritual before getting into bed was to say my prayers. Children said various prayers, but in my case it was:

> *Now I lay me down to sleep,*
> *I pray the Lord my soul will keep.*
> *If I should die before I wake,*
> *I pray the Lord my soul to take.*

The prayer was gabbled at a hundred miles an hour, and was bereft of all meaning, the main thing being to be able to say that you had done what was expected of you.

The board games that we played in the house were such old established favourites as Snakes and Ladders, Ludo, Tiddleywinks and Housey-housey. There was also a game called Escalado. This consisted of a length of tough material, which was about six inches wide. It was clamped to the table at one end, and the other was fastened by elastic to a ratchet device which was fitted with a handle which, when turned, caused the material to vibrate. Horses and jockeys made of lead were placed on the material at the start line, and they were vibrated to the finish line. It was an exciting game.

Card games were also popular, such as Snap, Rummy, Find the Lady and many others. Certainly, although we were poor, there was no shortage of things to do. My brother had a magic lantern for projecting images from slides onto a white sheet. A candle provided the light.

Christmas was always a very special time. Some time beforehand my parents would obligingly help me to write a letter to

Father Xmas, advising me what he would consider suitable presents. The letter was then 'posted' up one of the bedroom chimneys. On Christmas Eve I dutifully hung my pillowslip over the bedknob at the bottom of the bed, and vowed to keep awake to actually see Father Christmas arrive. However, sleep always won, and it was early morning when I opened my eyes, and there, to my delight, hung my pillowslip. But now it was not the limp thing from the previous night, but bulging with presents. What a wonderful feeling it was! In addition, all of the things that I had asked for were there, plus many others, such as an Annual, a compendium of games and so on.

Then came Christmas dinner. Usually this included turkey or chicken, things that were normally not on our menu. Both of my parents were superb cooks, so the meal was always a delight. Often there were even Christmas crackers, as well. How I loved Christmas!

At this time, all of my heroes were British, usually action men. At the top of my list was Captain Scott of the Antarctic and his companions, particularly Captain Oates. To me it seemed noble indeed to die whilst seeking glory for one's country, the more so when the ideals and goals were so pure.

A heroine with all schoolchildren, boys and girls, between the wars, was Nurse Edith Cavell. She lived in occupied territory during World War 1, and helped Allied prisoners to escape. She was executed by the German army in Brussels, on October 12th, 1915. The well known, poignant picture of her bravely facing the firing squad haunted my dreams on many nights.

Until the mid-1930's, when the area was demolished, my grandparents lived in old Douglas. They then went to live in Windsor Road with their two unmarried daughters. They must have liked living there, for that is where they stayed until they died. They had run it as a boarding house since they moved in, and this continued until after the war. In about 1953, the surviving family offered to sell it cheaply to me, but neither Pat, nor I had any desire to go into the boarding house business, so we declined their generous offer.

Therefore, this was the world, in which I grew up. There did not seem to be enough hours in the day to fit in all the things to do. It was a happy and carefree existence, surrounded by kind and loving people. I count myself lucky indeed to have had such a wonderful childhood.

CHAPTER FOUR

PLAYING, PLACES AND PASTIMES

Weeper, weeper, chimneysweeper.
Had a wife and couldn't keep her.

The games that we played depended largely upon the season, as you would expect. There was very little traffic in the avenue, so we had the place as a wonderful playground, almost for our exclusive use. Hillside Avenue is a cul-de-sac, the bottom being railed off by a wooden fence. The fence had an opening leading to a footpath, called the Cinder Path, which joined the avenue and Peel Road, adjacent to Belmont Hill. Because there was no through traffic, only a few delivery vans came along to interfere with our games, so it was perfectly safe.

Football, of course, was a popular winter game. The touch lines were the gutters, and the goals were coats laid on the ground. As with all the games that required two teams, we all lined up in front of the 'pickers', usually the best players at whatever game was to be played. The two pickers alternately selected one person for his team, and once selected we would stand behind the picker without a quibble. How soon you were selected was, of course, a measure of how valuable you were deemed to be to the team. With games like football there was no referee, so disputes were frequent, followed in due course by one side backing down, and the game would then recommence. Only boys were allowed to play rough games such as this. Usually, an old tennis ball was used as the football. On Saturday afternoons, though, we played at the Goose Neck, and used a proper ball. The Goose Neck was really the name of the track which joined Westmoreland Road, near Noble's Hospital, to Peel Road near Pulrose. But to us it was the extensive area of fields on either side of the track. Much of it was covered by gorse, so it was a popular place for courting couples in the summer. We played on the land at the top of the hill where the Ballabrooie houses now stand. The first houses were built about 1938, along with Ballakermeen School. As I recall, the houses cost about £200. Anyway, on the way home after the football, we would slide down the hill which faces the hospital, using a piece of wood, cardboard or corrugated iron for a slide. My favourite team at this time was Everton, and each week I read about their players, such as Dixie Dean and Tommy Lawton. To digress, I might mention that Ballakermeen School was completed just at the outbreak of the war. It was commandeered by the Royal Navy for use as a boy-entrant school, their base being at HMS St. George (Cunningham's Holiday Camp). It was returned to the Education Authority after the war, and became the first comprehensive school in the British Isles.

However, back to pre-war Hillside Avenue. In the evening playing was usually centered on the street lamp outside number twenty-four. The avenue was poorly lit, as the only other lamp posts were outside numbers twelve and thirty-six. A popular game was Hockey-go-Pushy. There were two teams, one on the road and the other on the pavement. At a given signal one person from the pavement team had to try to hop across the road, keeping one foot off the ground. Those in the middle, also hopping, had to try to make him put two feet on the ground. Everyone had to keep his arms folded across his chest, but barging and shoulder charging were permitted. If the one trying to cross put two feet on the groun he joined the other team. But, if he got acrtoss the road the rest of his team immediately tried to cross en masse. A similar game, but without hopping, was called Red Rover.

Another favourite was Kick the Tin.. One team had ten seconds to hide before the other team started to search for them. However, one boy stayed behind with his foot on a tin which was in the middle of the road. When someone hiding was found his name was called out loudly. He was then obliged to go to the 'den' alongside the tin. But, if one of the hiders could creep up unobserved to the tin and kick it away, then all those in the den were released and could hide again. We alsways hid in the gardens of houses, but only hid behind the front hedge, so did no damage.

CCK was a game that the girls also played. The initials stood for Chase, Catch, Kiss. The girls were given ten seconds to hide, and then the boys searched for them. They could kiss any girl that they found. Neeless to say, often the game did not last very long, because we would whisper to our favourite girl to hide in number so and so's garden. On the word 'go' we would home in like a guided missile to claim our kiss.

I have already mentioned the action of water on carbide when describing the acetylene bicycle lamp. Well this provided the basis of another exciting game. We would get a tin with a tight-fitting, push-on lid (a Bird's custard tin was ideal) and punch a hole in the base with a nail. A piece of carbide was placed in the tin and covered with spit, so releasing acetylene gas. The lid was put firmly on and the tin left on its side on the edge of the pavement for several seconds. A match was then applied to the hole, followed by a most gratifying explosion. The lid would be blown across the road. The beauty of this, though, was that one had merely to collect all the pieces and you were back in business again. No one ever tried to stop us playing the game, although the occupants of the nearby houses must certainly have heard the noise. For our part, we did not give a thought to the danger, which must have been quite considerable, had we stopped to think about it.

Then there was Alla-Balla. One boy (or girl) stood facing up the avenue, with his back to the other players. He threw a tennis ball backwards over his head and into the crowd. If it was caught by a girl she hid it in the leg of her knickers, if by a boy he put it up the back of his jumper. Once the ball had been hidden everyone chanted:

Alla-Balla, Alla-Balla, who's got the ball?
I haven't got it, and I haven't got it.
Alla-Balla, Alla-Balla, who's got the ball?

The thrower then had to guess which of the deliberately guilty looking players had it.

However, my favourite game of all was Soapy Soapsuds. I do not know how it got its name, but, as with most games, it required two teams. Wooden palings and privet hedges bounded the front gardens of the houses, and only boys could play. Those of one team bent down, legs apart and each boy in the team tucked his head between the legs of the one in front, making a line at right angles to the hedge. The front boy tucked his head down and clutched the palings. When the line was firmly established, there was a whoop of 'Soapy, Soapy Soapsuds!' from the other team. They raced across the road one after the other, and jumped on to the line of backs. Everyone had to get on, so you had to be sure that your best jumpers went first. The idea was to jump as high into the air as possible and land heavily, in an attempt to break the line of backs. When everyone was on, they had a further ten seconds to make the backs give way. Therefore, bouncing up and down was tried, as well as applying 'scissors' grips with the legs. If the backs gave way, they had to go down again. If not, then the other team was down.

Most games required two teams, so it was important that the picking was done to a ritual. In fact, there were rituals for almost all of our activities. It was all quite complicated, but it ensured that there was never a dispute about the outcome. Most of it is long forgotten, but I do remember one for determining who had first pick. All the participants stood in a circle with their clenched fists extended. Then one of the players (himself probably picked by some other ritual) tapped each fist in turn on each word of:

Your Bob owes my Bob two bob.
And, if your Bob doesn't give my Bob his two bob,
My Bob will give your Bob a bob in the eye.

The fist touched on the last word determined the chosen person, to the complete satisfaction of all concerned. By the way, 'bob' was slang for a shilling. Another ritual involved saying the well known, 'One potato, two potato, three potato, four....'

A pastime all the boys, and a few girls, enjoyed, involved placing a piece of wood on a roller skate to make a seat. Part way up the hill opposite number twelve, we would sit on the wood and career down the hill and onto the straight. Of course, we often fell off, so it was hard on our trousers. When the girls played on their own it was usually skipping, either individually or in a group, or doing handsprings against the wooden fence.

Skipping games were always popular with both girls and boys. The rope was a long length of clothesline turned by two people. The skipping was always done to a rhyme, such as:

*Mary in the kitchen,
Doing a bit of stitching.
Along comes the bogey man
And out goes she.*

On the last line, the girl who was skipping was replaced. Another song was:

*All in together now,
Never mind the weather now,
When I count twenty
The rope will be empty.
One, two, three... up to twenty*

As the words imply, everyone (maybe six or more people) would be skipping. The rope was turned very fast (a pepper) for the counting, and when it reached 'twenty' everyone dashed away. Another favourite started:

*On the mountain stands a lady,
Who she is I do not know.
Will she have me for a lover?
Will she answer 'yes' or 'no'?*

It went on for several more lines, but I can not recall them.

Sometimes the rope was just swayed to and fro, to a chant such as:

*Weeper, weeper, chimney sweeper,
Had a wife and couldn't keep her.
Had another, didn't love her.
Up the chimney, he did shove her.*

Yet another was:

> *Mickey Mouse had a house,*
> *What colour did he paint it?*
> *B. L. U. E. (or any other colour).*
> *Have you got it on you?*

Anyone wearing that colour joined the person skipping, and then called out the next colour. There were many more skipping songs, as it was such a popular pastime.

Then there was hopscotch. The road and pavements were covered with hopscotch beds, many of different layouts. They could be round, rectangular, spiral and probably others that I have forgotten. However, the most common layout was rectangular with a rounded top. A flat stone or a piece of slate was ideal for this game, as both would slide easily along the ground. The idea was to kick the stone whilst hopping on one foot. You could only put both feet on the ground at the rest bed, marked 'R'. The stone was kicked into each numbered square in turn. Care was taken to ensure that neither the stone nor your foot rested on any of the chalk lines. Neither could your stone touch anyone else's. Having completed the first round, you then missed bed number one, and proceeded as before. On the following round you missed bed one and two, and so on. Obviously, the game could last a long time. It was played all the year round by boys and girls, and had the great virtue that it could be played as a team or solo. Once you had drawn a bed, it was yours. No one would rub it out, but other people could play on it without your permission if you were not using it.

Sometimes if we became bored, we would play 'stooies'. This involved doing something that would annoy the residents, in the hope that they would chase us. For example, 'door knocking' consisted of tying a piece of dark cotton from the knocker of a house to our hiding place on the other side of the privet hedge. We would operate the knocker and, when the householder opened the door and closed it again, we would repeat the operation, and so on. On the other hand, this was such an established prank that often the irate householder would rush out of the house to where he knew we were hiding, and we would run like the wind. Anyone caught would get his ears boxed, and this was accepted as part of the game. A variation of this game was to tie the knockers of adjacent houses together, and then knock on both doors. This was not very popular, though, because we lost a long length of valuable string each time. There was quite a hierarchy of houses, which were fair game. Thus, all the houses of the children were exempt, as were those of people that we particularly liked, such as Killey's, Kermode's and Cooile's. Then there were the houses where someone was ill. So, there were not many houses that were fair game. One was number twenty-five, that belonging to Mr. Hales. We door-tapped his house regularly, usually with no response. However, one night, almost as a routine, we tapped his house again. He must have been waiting for us, for no sooner had we started than the door flew open and he tore out of the house after us. He took us all by surprise, not least because we did not realise that he could run so fast. Several of us got a thick ear from him, and it became something of a badge of honour to say that he had given you a clout.

We never did any damage to property, nor was anything stolen. Most of the houses had unlocked doors, so we could have walked in at any time. In my own house, the back door key had been lost for several years, and it was about 1950 before my father decided that it was time to replace it. By that time, we lived in number twenty-six, but it did not have a back door key either.

The avenue had more than its fair share of interesting people. The Shimmin family lived in number twenty. There were three girls and one boy, Sidney. During the war, he was a Spitfire pilot. Later, he rose through the ranks of the Steam Packet to become its General Manager. His eldest sister Gladys had a boarding house on Queen's Promenade and the other girls were twins called Ena and Winnie.

Jack Christian was another resident. He was a fine singer and was in great demand as an entertainer all over the Island. The Addison family lived just across the road from him. Mrs. Addison was a gentle and kindly, grey haired woman. She had sons called George and Arthur, and a daughter, Lydia. They were all older than I was, so I had little contact with them. However, during the war George joined the army as a private, and was demobilised as a major, which was a fine tribute to both him and his family. Understandably, his mother was very proud of him.

The Kermode family lived next door to me, in number twenty-nine, and their son, Frank, served in the Royal Navy during the war, after which he went to university. After graduation he became a Professor of English, and has appeared many times on the television in highbrow discussion programmes. He was knighted a few years ago.

Marshall Killey who lived in number twenty-seven (the boy who could drive a lorry when he was about thirteen) served his apprenticeship at Shimmin's garage on Queen's Promenade. Later he went on, I believe, to become the Chief Driving Examiner for the Island.

Arthur Adams lived three doors down from me. He was a little older than I was, and he had a great gift for story telling. We would all sit on the pavement with our backs to the railings, outside number twenty-four where the lamp was, and Arthur would tell us thrilling tales. He would stride up and down as though he was on a stage, and we all listened with rapt attention. I do not know where he learned these tales, but never once did he repeat a story. I lost contact with him for many years, and I always thought that he must have gone into show business, as he was so good. In the event, though, he served in the Merchant Navy. He had relatives who lived further along the avenue called Kewley. There were two boys, Harry, who was about my age, and Kenneth. Harry and I were quite friendly, and he joined the RAF and became a bomb aimer. I only saw him once in his uniform, and that was at the Villa Marina, early in 1943. He looked fine, and I envied him. On Christmas Eve that same year, his mother was notified that he had been killed whilst on an operation. A poem was published in the Manx paper about his last flight.

Mr Killip lived in number two. This is a corner house, so has a large garden. He seemed to spend all of his spare time gardening, and it was a showpiece. Today it would surely be eligible to be featured on the television. No one even dreamed of doing any damage to it.

A classmate called Geoffrey Corlett lived in number twelve. His father drove a beautiful, horse-drawn baker's cart. The cart was a large, box-like structure, painted black with red and gold trimmings, and it gleamed under several coats of varnish. It was always in pristine condition, and drawn by a magnificent brown horse which had highly polished harness and brasses. Mr. Corlett sat atop the cart, and the whole effect was magnificent. I used to wish so hard that I could ride up there with the driver. However, Mr. Corlett did not seem to be a very approachable man, so I never got the chance. One winter's evening, though, a motor car collided with the horse and cart, killing Mr. Corlett and his horse.

The Pease family had two sons, Bert and Lionel. Bert was involved in a tragic accident whilst playing in Port-e-Chee meadow with a neighbour. His playmate was swinging a golf club, and caught Bert in the face, with the result that Bert lost the sight of one eye. This was a tragic accident to happen to anyone, but was singularly sad to happen to such a young boy.

The family of Ken Quane, who is now a well-known local preacher, moved into number thirty-one in 1939. Another person who became well known is David Byrne. He lived in his grandma's house (Mrs. Varley, number forty-two). David, and his equally talented wife,

Nancy, are two of the foremost painters on the Island.

Then there was the lodger in our house, George Broad, the very well known pianist. David Byrne has told me that he used to stand outside my house and listen to George playing. George performed several sell-out concerts at the Gaiety, one of his showstoppers being The Ritual Fire Dance.

Perhaps I may even presume to include myself. In 1953 I graduated from engineering college, and became a Chartered Engineer, which entitles me to put C. Eng., M I E E, M I Mech. E after my name. I had a technical book published in 1984, and the print-run was sold out very quickly.

Although I never knew him, John Parkinson, the Mayor of Douglas in about 1973, lived in number twenty-three.

A regular playmate of mine was Percy Daugherty. He and I often went about together, and one summer afternoon we were on one of the small jetties that ran at right angles from the promenade. As it was covered at high tide, the surface was covered in seaweed and slime. Suddenly, and without warning, Percy fell into the water. I promptly lay on the slime and grabbed his hand, but I could not get enough purchase to pull him out. In fact, because of the slime, he was slowly and remorselessly ensuring that I would join him. It was just getting to the stage where I had to decide whether to get a wetting or to let him go for a moment, whilst I moved to a new position. However, it was not necessary, for a visitor in a rowing boat came to my friend's aid and helped him out. We went home, Percy dripping wet. This was not unusual for boys - normally because they had fallen into the boating pool, in the sunken gardens.

Death was ever present. The Johnson's lived in number fifty-one, and had several children. Proudly displayed in the hall of their house was a large model of the Mona's Queen, which had been made by Mr. Johnson. It was about four feet long and was very good. Sadly, he died very suddenly, and one can only speculate about the terrible problems that this must have caused the family.

The Jewel family lived in number thirty, and they had two daughters, Margaret and Annie. Annie was my age, but she died in 1936. I do not remember what the cause was, but it was probably tuberculosis, the dreaded TB. Four of us knocked on Mrs. Jewel's door and asked whether we could see Annie. We were led upstairs to the bedroom where she lay. She looked serene and, except that she was so pale, it was difficult to realise that she was dead. Hers was the first corpse that I had ever seen. However, there were several deaths in the avenue among the young people from either TB or the equally feared diphtheria, which were both killer diseases. Whenever you heard that so and so had been taken to the White Hoe (the isolation hospital) suffering from TB or 'Dip' you knew that there was a good chance that you might not see them again. Tom Quane, who moved into number thirty-one in 1939, drove the fever ambulance. Amongst the deaths were those of Kathleen Brady and her sister, Patsy, two very popular girls. Another was Joan McConvey. Incidentally, many years later, Emmy, my sister in law, married Joan's father.

When someone died, the female neighbours would lay out the body. One person in the avenue who was renowned for her 'laying out' skills was Hetty Kinrade from number forty-three. The procedure involved washing the body and making the corpse presentably attired. The body was laid on a bed until the coffin was ready. At the time that the funeral procession was due to set off, the downstairs curtains or blinds in every house in the avenue were drawn until the hearse had passed. The funeral cortege moved at walking pace all the way to the church and then to the cemetery. All pedestrians stood still as the procession passed, and men removed their headgear. It was always regarded as most important that everyone showed proper respect for the dead, even if they had no idea whose funeral it was.

Although we were saddened by young deaths, it did not interfere with the seasonal round of games. Some, like skipping, were played in summer and winter, but others were particular to a season. During the summer cricket was popular. The garden gate of a house was the wicket, the edge of the pavement the crease, and the opposite pavement edge was the bowling crease. A tennis ball was used and, if the batsman missed the ball, he was almost certainly out. One summer my brother George set up something of a cricket record. He broke a window in Mrs. Kermode's house one week, a window in our house the following week and one in Mrs. Killey's the next. Three windows in three weeks! The replacement glass for a window cost 7/6d, (36p) so my father was not exactly pleased with George's record, particularly as he also had to fit the glass himself.

One thing that surprises me when I look back is that when Test matches were being played, I always supported Australia rather than England. Of course, Australia was a part of the Empire, so it was not treasonable, but it was certainly odd. I knew all the top players of the time such as Verity, Bradman, Ponsford, Ames and so on, from cigarette cards.

Playing 'ciggy cards' was another favourite summer game. Each packet of twenty cigarettes contained two cards. With the large number of visitors to Douglas in the summer, it was easy to accumulate a large hoard. All that was required was to stand at the foot of the Falcon Cliff incline railway, where there was a battery of cigarette machines on the road leading to the promenade. There was a continuous stream of young men using the incline, coming from Cunningham's Holiday Camp. Many of them would stop to use the machines, and most of them would give the cards away. The cigarettes cost eleven and halfpenny a packet. You put a shilling in the machine, and the halfpenny change was in the packet. The game of ciggy cards was very simple. Two players knelt on the edge of the pavement and flicked the cards one at a time in turn toward the railings. This went on until one of the cards landed on another, so winning all the cards that had been thrown.

At the time of the TT and the MPG, hoop running was all the go. The hoop was usually an old pram wheel with a stiff wire handle. We would chase up and down the avenue, having previously established which of our favourites we were, such as Jimmy Guthrie, Stanley Woods, Freddie Frith and so on. Sometimes a boy was lucky enough to get a metal numberplate from one of the riders, and it would be worn with pride. It was even better if you could get one of the cloth numbers that the riders wore on their back, with cross-over white tapes, tied at the front. Having one of these guaranteed you star status. Similarly, when the Mannin Beg and Mannin Mooar motor car races were held, we would tear up and down the road pulling tin motor cars by a string. Most of them had been bought in Woolworth's, usually several years earlier, as the clockwork motors had long before broken. The cars were often of German manufacture, and on the inside of the metal you could see the names of the original contents of the tins from which they had been made, such as salmon. The real races gave us the chance to see all the top drivers of the day, such as Kay Don, Freddie Dixon, Prince Bira of Siam and many others. Part of the circuit was down Summer Hill, along the promenade to Greensill's Corner (at the end of Castle Street), where they doubled back and turned left up Broadway. I always thought these races were even better than the TT.

Fishing was always popular, although we never caught anything. We did not have a rod, just a length of line and a hook. The first stop was the fish market where we would ask for some bait. Then it was on to the swing bridge, where we ducked under the turnstile when the man in the pay hut was not looking - or so we thought. After that, we called at the Lifeboat House, overlooked by the Fort Anne Hotel where Sir William Hillary, the founder of the Lifeboat Institution, once lived. He was instrumental in having the Tower of Refuge built in 1832, after having been involved in several rescues from ships wrecked on the rocks. However, our real destination was the Blackboards, which run beside the Battery Pier, facing the Croagh. We hopefully dangled the bait in the water, but I can not recollect ever getting a single bite. But, this did not matter, as we enjoyed ourselves. We never did stupid things with the line and hook, although one time my brother George managed to get a hook stuck in his tongue. I was not present, so I do not know the details. Fortunately, the others did not try to get the hook out. Instead, they took George to the newspaper shop that Mr. Jewel (from number thirty-one) had at the corner of Walpole Avenue. He cut the end of the hook off, and passed the rest of it through George's tongue, so no harm was done.

Having unsuccessfully dabbled our lines in the water for, maybe, two or three hours, at ten minutes to four it was forgotten completely. We would make a mad dash to the elevated part at the end of the pier, near the little lighthouse. There followed one of the most exciting sights that I can remember as a child. Six or more ships of the Steam Packet fleet were moored (often one alongside the other, as there were so many of them) at the Victoria Pier. Each ship would be full of holidaymakers returning home. At five minutes to four, they each sounded their whistles one after the other. I suppose there must have been some order of priority in this, as no two whistles were ever sounded together. We quickly learned how to identify a ship from the sound of its whistle, even when it was moored on the far side of the pier, and only the ship's superstructure could be seen. The King Orry posed no problem at all, for, unlike the others, it did not have a deep throated sound like a fog horn, but a destroyer's siren that gave a high pitched shriek that went 'whoop, whoop'. Incidentally, this was the only merchant ship present at the surrender of the German fleet at Scapa Flow in 1918. All the ships had good Manx names, such as Lady of Mann; Ben my Chree; Mona's Queen (destined to be sunk at the mole at Dunkirk, whilst participating in the evacuation); Manxman; Manxmaid; Viking; Rushen Castle and so on. In 1938, two more ships joined the fleet, the Tynwald and the Fenella. They were beautiful vessels, but, sadly, were sunk during the war. But, in those magic days before the war, the sight of all those ships was a joy to behold. At exactly four o'clock each ship played follow-my-leader astern out of the harbour. We waved like mad from the pier as the ships passed, and the visitors waved back. I suppose it was an adventure for them, just as it was for us. Once clear of the harbour the ships would stop and then start powering forward to destinations with names such as Ardrossan; Liverpool; Siloth; Fleetwood; Heysham; Dublin; Belfast et cetera. We stared at them until they became little more than spots on the water, and finally they were lost from sight. That was the signal to start making our way home, the end of another good day's fishing. Before the war, the three 'white boats' were particularly impressive. They were the Mona's Queen, Lady of Mann and Ben my Chree. Each of them had its funnel painted in the standard black and red, but the hull and superstructure was painted brilliant white, down to the water line. Below that, they were painted green, so they looked absolutely spick and span. However, the cost of maintaining such a livery was such that after the war they reverted to the standard colours.

Sometimes when we went fishing, we could travel in style on one of the three steam ferries that plied between the Victoria and Battery Piers. They were called the Shamrock, Rose and Thistle. Oliver McGrath's father worked on the Rose, so if this one was in service we could have a free ride. The ferries did a roaring business, particularly in the morning, and it was heaven to glide across the still water. Each one had a musician on board, so as the vessel moved effortlessly across the harbour, the splendid violin playing of Tony Ventro could be heard or tinkling piano music. The visitors were not going fishing, of course. They were making their way to Douglas Head. It was a steep climb from the pier, made more manageable by the various stalls on the right hand side from the pier to the bottom of the incline railway. One particular stall that I remember had a weighing arrangement mounted on a brass tripod. The person to be weighed sat in a chair, whilst the showman made a fine display of placing the highly polished brass weights on the pan.

The steam ferries sailed from the Victoria Pier to the Battery Pier, and did a roaring business, particularly in the morning. Out of the three, the Rose, Thistle and Shamrock, two were in service at any one time. (Courtesy of the Terry Faragher Collection)

*The three 'white boats' were a fine sight between the wars. They were the Lady of Mann; the Mona's Queen and the Ben my Chree. The Mona's Queen was mined and sank off the mole at Dunkirk on May 29 1940. Twenty-four of her crew died.
(Courtesy of the Terry Faragher Collection)*

At the bottom of the incline railway was a small amusement arcade. It was not the seedy sort of thing that one associates with such places today, but a happy, open and carefree place where children could mingle with the crowd without the slightest worry. In fact, my wife, when a young girl, was employed there to give change, usually six pennies for a sixpence piece. It was here that the visitors had to make up there minds whether to climb the remainder of the way, or let the train take the strain by going up in style on the incline railway. I think it cost a halfpenny. There were two cars; one at the top and the other at the bottom, each joined by a wire rope, so as one went up the other coming down assisted it. Business was brisk, but during the war it fell into disrepair, so presumably it was too expensive to return it to service.

Once at the top there were various interesting things to do. One of them was to visit the Camera Obscura. It is still there, one of the few left in the British Isles. After the war it fell into a state of disrepair, and was in danger of being scrapped. However, the Manx Government has now stepped in, so this delightful building's future should now be assured. Once inside, there is a series of whitewashed tabletops, and on to each, a picture of the surrounding area is projected from a lens in the roof. Sometimes there would be a bottleneck at one of the pictures if it happened to be showing an oblivious courting couple, stealing what they thought was a secret kiss. The pictures were all excellent, particularly those of the sea and cliffs. Everyone should visit it at least once. The quotation from Keats, displayed outside the building, is apposite; 'A thing of beauty is a joy for ever.'

There was also the Minstrel Show. This was an open-air theatre, and there were about six performers. The posh seats at the front were deck chairs, whilst further back were wooden forms. In addition, you could stand outside the low wall, which surrounded the seating area. Although there was no admission charge, you were expected to contribute when the man came round with the collection tin. This, of course, did not apply to us children, so we had the best of all worlds, as we could watch the show for nothing without any feelings of guilt.

Another 'must' in the area was a visit to the lighthouse. In the wintertime its six flashes followed by six dark periods was a sombre, but reassuring sight. However, on a lovely summer day it was an exciting place to visit. The keeper would show the visitors around, and always made a point of telling everyone that the heavy mirror arrangement floated on a pool of mercury. Everyone seemed duly impressed by this, although they had no means of knowing whether it was true or not - it is, in fact.

Those visitors with money to spend could travel along the Marine drive on the electric tram to Port Soderick. I so wished that I knew someone who worked on the railway, so that I could have a free ride, but sadly, I did not, so I could not. It must have been a spectacular ride, as the line hugged the side of the rocks, sometimes going over enormous trestle bridges. Upon arrival at Port Soderick, one made the descent to the shoreline by means of yet another funicular railway. When I come to think of it, there were quite a few funiculars at that time, but now they have all gone, the one from Falcon Cliff being the last. It remained until the 1990's. To me, there was nothing much to do when one got to Port Soderick, but it must have had some appeal for the visitors, as it was a very popular place to visit. Alternative ways to travel were by either the steam train or by sea. Various fishing boats were used for the sea journey, plus one outstanding boat that was tailor-made for the trip, the Karina. This small vessel's hull was painted brilliant white, and the woodwork of the deck and open-air seating shone under several coats of varnish. The finishing touch of this beautiful ship was the fawn-painted funnel. Again, how I wished that I could have a trip on this fairy-tale ship! I can still recall the thrill I experienced, whilst watching from Douglas Head, as the Karina made its stately progress past the lighthouse on a flat calm sea towards Port Soderick. In the 1960's, I

The Douglas Head Railway, which ran to Port Soderick, via the spectacular Marine Drive.

visited the Island with my young children, and there, lying-up in Douglas harbour, was the Karina, but by then in a sadly dilapidated state.

The film No Limit was made in 1936, much of it shot on the Island, so it provided much excitement for us. George Formby and Florence Desmond headed the cast. They were two of the top stars of the time. It was interesting to watch the scenes being shot, as this was the first chance we had ever had to watch a film being made. The actors looked quite off-putting, as they had to wear yellow make-up. It seems that yellow shows up as white on black and white film. I recall one scene being shot at the War Memorial in Douglas, which involved the stars. I was amazed at the number of times that they did the same little scene, particularly as it did not even get into the finished picture. For those scenes that involved the TT grandstand, anyone could join the crowd to make the stand look full. My mother was in the crowd for one day's shooting, for which, in addition to being able to say that she had appeared in a film, she, and all the others in the crowd, was given a bottle of pop, i.e., mineral water. However, nowadays it has all changed out of recognition. For example, Quintin's wife, Joy, and their daughter, Laura, have both appeared as extras in films, for which they received fifty pounds per session, plus meals. Several films are being made on the Island, so there is also a big demand for extras.

Unlike today, parents seemed to be unconcerned if we went missing, assuming that they had even noticed that we were, in the first place. For example, one day I left my house in the morning during the summer holidays, to play in the street. I met some boys who were going to visit a farm near Crosby, and they invited me along. So off I went, without giving a thought to telling my mother where I was going - I just went. It was about seven o'clock in the evening when I returned home, and when my mother saw me she just said,"Your dinner's in the oven." She did not even bother to ask me where I had been. Our parents had no need to worry anyway, as we never caused trouble, nor did we get into any. Moreover, the adults with whom we came into contact did not interfere with us in any way. We might have lacked sophistication, but we seemed to make up for it in innocence.

If two or three of us had a penny or two to spend, we would go to Onchan Head. To get there we would jog along the promenade, keeping pace with a horse tram. The trams were usually crowded, and often the passengers would be having a fine time singing songs such as Sons of the Sea, and bobbing up and down at the appropriate time. To me, Onchan Head seemed to be a wonderland. There was the Ghost Train, Hall of Mirrors, the Tunnel of Love, Figure of Eight and many other large amusements. In addition, there were the smaller, but still exciting, things to do, such as the slot machines, housey-housey (bingo), What the Butler Saw, Hoop-la and so on. Of course, we could only afford to go on a slot machine, but it was nice to see the visitors enjoying themselves. Sometimes they would let us play the last ball on a pintable, or throw the last hoop on the hoop-la stall. Also amongst the amusements were the forerunners of the jukeboxes. There were three of them, each in an identical blue cabinet, which stood about three feet tall. Attached to each was a thing like a stethoscope. Having selected your tune, you listened to it through the earpieces. Once, a visitor left a machine running, so I was able to hear the last part of 'I Left my Heart in Heidelberg With You, Dear'. The music was very 'tinny', and it is strange how I can still hear the music. At tea time we would head for home, again jogging along the promenade, and keeping going until we reached Hillside Avenue.

Without any prompting, the games that we played changed. At one time marbles was all the go, and then suddenly it was conkers, or some other game. Marbles was played in the gutter, and the ritual involved names such as Knuckle-Down-Tight, Big Man, Little Man and many others. I often wonder what happened to all those marbles. We all had so many, that surely we should now be walking on a carpet of them. They were almost all made of glass, so they cannot have just faded away.

A 'Stranraer' flying boat was moored in Douglas harbour in 1935. It was the most exciting aircraft that I had ever seen, and resulted in me volunteering for aircrew when I joined the RAF.
(Courtesy of the Terry Faragher Collection)

One day in 1935 an event occurred that was to profoundly alter my life. An RAF Stranraer flying boat landed in Douglas harbour, and was moored at the Croagh, near the lifeboat slipway. The endurance of the aircraft was 10 hours, and its speed was 165 mph. At that time, it had only recently entered RAF service. During the war, Sunderland's superseded it. However, this Stranraer was here, now. To me it was the most wonderful aircraft that I had ever seen. I stared at it for ages, and my imagination ran riot as I thought how exciting it would be to fly in such a magnificent machine. As a result, I had a deep desire to fly in the RAF, although in my heart I realised that my chances of actually doing so were just about zero; but anyway, I could dream.

Meanwhile, life went on. If the weather was nice during the summer holidays we would sometimes go swimming in the sea, or rather, play about in the water. It may seem strange, but most of us could not swim. When we had splashed about for a while, we quit the beach and made our way to either Feldman's or Lawrence Wright's. They were music publishers and, to help their sales of popular music along, they each had a large hall, one in Strand Street and one in Castle Street. The halls were bare, except for a grand piano, mounted on a moveable platform. Also on the platform was an easel, fastened to which were many sheets, on each of which the words of a popular tune was printed in large letters. At the start of a session, the platform was pushed to the front of the empty hall, almost to the street. The pianist would rattle off some popular tunes, and the men, who were later to sell the sheet music and the songbooks, would sing along. Soon a small crowd of holidaymakers would be singing along, and the platform moved back a little. As more people joined in, the platform was moved further back, and so on, until the hall was full in next to no time. The visitors were quite uninhibited, and sang along with gusto. Therefore, this is where we were heading for, after the beach.

Although the singsong was our destination, we would usually stop off at Gore's rock shop, for outside stood a young girl, holding a tray of broken rock. It was her job to offer pieces to the passers-by. We would try to creep up on her and grab some rock or, if she was friendly, just help ourselves. Then it was on to the singsong. We knew every word of every song that was being 'pushed' in the hall, and joined in wholeheartedly. We always stood against the wall and never caused any trouble, so we were never ejected. The song pluggers worked very hard, as they had to sing along, do solo turns, carry out comic banter, circulate amongst the crowd selling the music and always be very cheerful. In Feldman's, the pianist was a large, middle-aged woman. She was very jolly, and it was rumoured that she was the sister of Florrie Ford, one of the greatest entertainers of the time. I have no means of knowing whether this was true or not. Along with sheet music, the Little Blue Book was sold. These books cost sixpence, and contained the lyrics of a hundred popular songs of the day. They were in great demand, particularly as the songs were those being plugged. I remember such numbers as Happy Days Are Here Again; Goodnight My Love; Goody-Goody; The Glory of Love; September in the Rain, and many more. Certainly, Douglas was a crowded, happy and lively place in the summer.

Flat-topped straw hats were popular with the smart young men, up to the outbreak of war. Such a hat was called a straw cady, and for some unknown reason, this involved a little ritual with us. Each time we saw one, we would touch our tongue with our right thumb-tip, touch the middle of the left palm with the right thumb, circle the left hand and finally touch the left palm with the right fist. If there were two or more straw cadies the left palm was circled the appropriate number of times. The procedure probably sounds very complicated, but it is not really. Try it.

On Sunday mornings a pilgrimage for the visitors was to go to the morning open-air service at Braddan Church. The congregation often numbered several thousand, and the service was held in the field

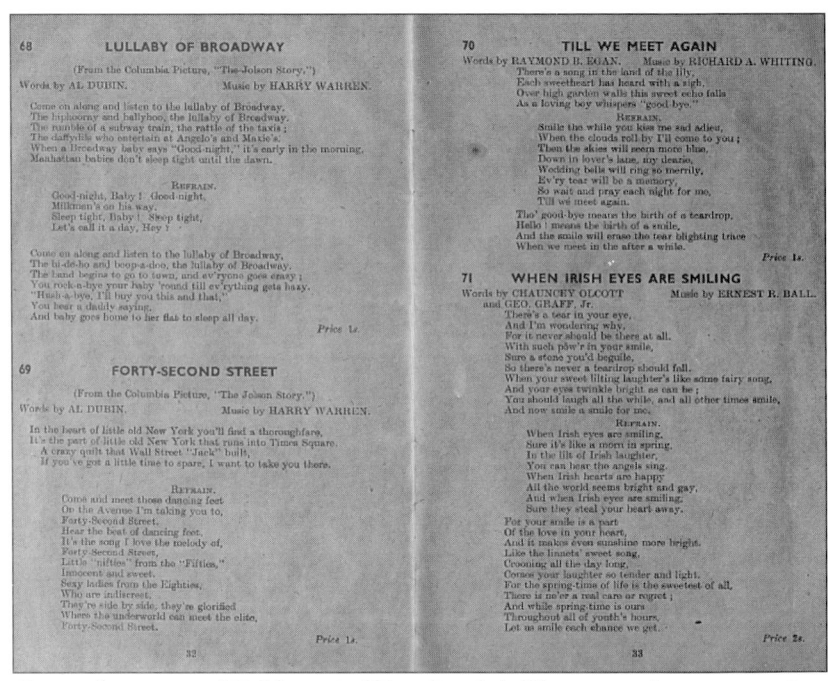

Pages from one of Feldman's 'Blue Books'. They cost sixpence, and had the words of 100 songs. They were very popular with the visitors. Lawrence Wright's had a similar book, but theirs had a brown cover.

adjacent to the church. For a couple of hours before the service there was a constant stream of people making their way along the Peel Road to Braddan. The alternative was to go by train. The Isle of Man Railway was in its heyday at that time, with services to Peel, Port Erin and Ramsey. If in the vicinity of the railway station, we made a point of going on to the platform to wave to the trains as they departed. Incidentally, the abattoir was situated near the station, so it was a common sight to see the cows and other animals being walked along Peel Road to the slaughterhouse.

The old Red Pier was being transformed into the King Edward Pier in the 1930's. For driving the piles for the extension, there was a ship called the Rock Breaker. Much of the work involved divers, and it was interesting to watch them. The old diving suits were very cumbersome and included heavy boots and a heavy helmet. The helmet was a large, brass affair, and had air hoses connected to it. Air was supplied from a crude-looking pump, operated by two men who turned the handles very casually. Although I felt that it would be exciting to be a diver, I also feared that the men doing the pumping would decide to have a rest, and leave me to die below the surface. On one occasion, my mother was invited to have tea with the captain on the Rock Breaker, and she took me along. I was, therefore, able to see over this interesting ship, and I was most surprised to see how clean and comfortable the cabin was in which we dined. I felt very special. If you watch No Limit, some of the scenes were shot on Douglas Head, and, in the background, you can see the work on the new pier in progress. The pier was completed in 1938. In the same shots you can see the old Victoria Pier Arcade, surmounted by the magnificent clock tower, but now replaced by the Terminal Buildings.

There were flagpoles at regular intervals all the way from the Victoria Pier to the War Memorial, from which the flags of the nations were flown. Today the same few flags are repeated, but before the war, each was different. It was a source of pride if you could name every one of the countries represented, such as Estonia,

Lithuania, Fiji and Japan, even if you knew little or nothing about them.

    A trip could be had in a superb speedboat called 'I'm Alone', for about 2/6d. This was quite expensive, but it must have been a thrilling ride. The trip started from the Victoria Pier, and once in the bay the boat would roar at full speed toward the Onchan Head end and back again, the bow high in the air and the Red Ensign flying straight out from the stern. It looked magnificent. An equally exciting trip was in an amphibian aircraft, called the Cloud of Iona. It carried about six passengers, which, on one trip, included my mother. Somehow, she had saved the fare of five shillings for this once-in-a-lifetime trip. The aircraft landed on the water and then taxied onto the sand. A trip lasted about twenty minutes, and involved flying around Douglas and nearby places. Mother was thrilled with the ride, and felt that it was well worth the huge expenditure.

    All the factories in a particular area of Britain closed for the annual holidays at the same time. For example, in July, there was 'Scotch Week', and Douglas was full of happy Scots. A highlight of that week was the Highland Games, which was held in the Nunnery grounds. All the usual events were staged, such as tossing the caber. On one occasion, so I have been informed, a tree was cut down and trimmed to the required size for the event. But, when the burly Scot who was to do the tossing tried to lift it, he could not budge it. It seems that the caber should be made from wood that has been thoroughly dried, but this had not been done to this one. It retained its moisture, probably doubling its weight! The beauty of the Gathering was that, from my bedroom window, I had an uninterrupted view of the clearing where many of the events took place. I could not make out much detail, but it was certainly a colourful spectacle. Many of the spectators wore full highland dress, and I used to wonder how they could carry such an elegant but heavy costume, besides their ordinary clothes, in just the two suitcases that were the norm. My eldest brother, Ernie, worked at the Nunnery. He was the chauffeur /

The amphibian, 'Cloud of Iona', in which my mother had a memorable flight around Douglas for five shillings. Another aircraft, which provided similar flights, was the 'Cutty Sark'.
(Courtesy of the Terry Faragher Collection)

The speedboat, 'I'm Alone', was a very popular attraction. It was owned and operated by Walter and Fred Hawley. They also had an electrical business, and traded as 'Hawley Brothers, Electricians'. Walter installed the first bed radios in Noble's Hospital.
(Courtesy the Hawley family.)

mechanic, and looked super in his uniform of peaked cap, high-buttoned jacket, breeches and leather leggings. He drove and maintained an immaculate silver Rolls Royce. As he worked there, I was able to see around the house. I was most impressed by the large number and size of the rooms, and how opulently they were furnished. I felt it would be rather nice to live in such a place.

In the evening you could walk along many of the streets near Strand Street, and hear singing all the way. Every pub seemed to have a singing licence, so the customers had a good bawling session. As the sound from one pub died away, that of the next would be heard. I expect it was the usual beery stuff, but I thought it was jolly, and longed for the day when I would be old enough to join in. One pub in particular that I recall is the Adelphi, which stood at the bottom of Police Station Hill.

There were hundreds of comic postcards, and I think I knew almost every one. They were usually displayed on large boards outside the shops, so you could browse through them at your leisure. The cards were censored, so were rude rather than vulgar. There is now a large collection of this type of card available for viewing in the Manx Museum library. The usual type of comic card would show, say, a large woman (all comic card women were huge, except for their very trim daughters) hanging a large pair of bloomers on the washing line, and prominently displayed alongside was a pair of very stylish briefs. The neighbour was leaning over the fence, saying 'I see your daughter's come home, then'. To me, this kind of thing was hilarious.

The Manx Grand Prix races marked the end of the holiday season, after which we quickly settled down to the winter routine again. The cinema was a prime source of entertainment. The very first film that I saw was called Trader Horn, at the Picture House. My dad took me to see it, and I seem to remember him saying either that it was the first all-talking picture, or that it was the first talking picture to be shown on the Island. Whichever it was, the only thing that I can remember about it is the title. Later, though, going to the pictures was, for me, an important part of my life. I attended St. Matthew's Sunday School in the afternoon and, in the evening, I reluctantly went to that service with my parents. As a sop to make me feel better about going, my father would promise to give me sixpence to go to the pictures afterwards. This helped enormously. The service started at six-thirty and the pictures at eight o'clock, so normally there was no conflict between them. However, sometimes during the sermon the vicar would ramble on interminably. In desperation, I would keep asking Dad what time it was, and groan as it got nearer and nearer to the magic hour of eight o'clock. When it got to five minutes to the hour he would give in, and give me the sixpence. I would make a hurried and undignified exit from the church, and run all the way to the Strand Cinema, where the Gene Autrey films were shown.

If I did not go to the Strand, it had to be the Royalty in Walpole Avenue, as these were the only ones that you could get in for sixpence. The other two that were open in the winter, were the Picture House and the Regal, each of which charged an extortionate nine-penny minimum, so was quite out of the question. I suppose you paid the extra admission because each had a magnificent electric organ, which rose out of a pit in the floor, rather like a space ship taking off. The one at the Regal always seemed better to me, but both were beautifully illuminated and the colours changed continuously. I marvelled at how the organist was able to play, using both hands on the massive keyboards, selecting the correct stops out of the huge number available, and all the time his feet danced up and down on the foot pedals. It was even more complicated as the organ rose or descended, for in addition to his other accomplishments, he now had to continue playing whilst he twisted round to face the audience. Certainly, the spectacle gave a sense of occasion to a visit to the cinema. I can not recall the name of the organist at the Picture House, but the one at the Regal was Dr. Tootall. Every time I went to the Regal he played a delightful tune called 'I've Got It Bad And That Ain't Good', so it must have been a favourite of his, as it is with me.

I sang (not very well) in the choir at St. Matthew's. My eldest brother, Ernie, served on the altar. Here we are about 1936, outside the church.

However, this was still in the future. My Sunday visits cost sixpence because there was no half price. For the rest of the week, though, children were admitted for half price if accompanied by an adult. To circumvent this we employed a system that many modern social workers might find hair-raising. With the three pence I had been given to go to the pictures, usually in the winter, I would stand outside the Royalty. As soon as a man appeared on his own, fumbling in his pocket for a sixpence, I would say, 'Take me in mister?' and offer him the three pence. Almost invariably, he would do so, so I was in. Once inside I thanked him and left him. Now, why did this happen at the Royalty? Because the toilets were at the rear, and to get to them it was necessary to go past the nine pence seats. Therefore, on my return from the toilet I would sit in one of these posh seats. I always felt that this little manoeuvre passed unnoticed, but in reality, I expect the attendants had a good laugh at my expense. A secondary, but good, reason for choosing the Royalty was that this was where the Gainsborough films were shown, and they had many fine artists, such as Will Hay. I used to roar with laughter at his antics and those of his companions, Moore Marriott and Graham Moffit. At this time, all the cinemas had two continuous performances each weekday evening. The show started at six-thirty, and typically comprised a short film, such as a Travelogue or a Laurel and Hardy, a newsreel (Pathe Gazette at the Royalty and the Regal, Movietone News at the other two), plus a cartoon, and sometimes a comedy 'Our Gang' film. The leader of the gang of children was called Spanky Macfarland, and the only other gang member that I can recall is Buckwheat. The feature film followed. All this in a cosy and warm cinema with comfortable seats was excellent value for money. It certainly provided an escape from the grinding toil of so many people's lives.

On Friday (payday) my mother always went shopping in the evening, the shops being open until about ten o'clock. I loved going into places such as the Maypole, Home and Colonial and Lipton's. The Maypole sold butter, cheese and other dairy products. The shop had a tiled floor, upon which fresh sawdust was scattered each day, so there was always a lovely cut-wood smell which mingled with that of the huge slabs of butter and cheese. If you ordered say, a pound of Empire butter, the assistant would cut a rectangular slab of the required weight from the larger slab, using wooden butter pats. The piece was put on greaseproof paper to be weighed, and he, or she, had a small extra piece in case it was needed. Usually it was not, as the estimate had been spot on. I never remember an assistant having to go back for more. Their excellent estimate of the required weight was amazing. Once the correct weight was obtained the butter was patted into its final shape and the pattern applied. The paper was then folded around it as quickly and perfectly as if done by a machine. The whole operation was carried out at lightening speed, usually whilst the assistant carried on a lively conversation with the customer. Nowadays this would make an excellent item for a TV game show. Lipton's and the Home and Colonial were both grocery shops, but their assistants were equally talented, but now they performed with rice, sugar and lentils. They could estimate the weight to a tiny fraction of an ounce, and seal the stiff, blue-paper bags neatly and at astonishing speed.

There were two large, adjacent toyshops in Strand Street, called Johnson's and Sisson's. Each had large, curved windows, and a wonderful display of toys. I do not know how they kept going, as the toys were expensive, so there could not have been a great demand, but it was heaven just to stare and dream about the ones that I most coveted. When I look back, dreaming formed a large part of our lives. There were so many things that we would like to have had, but could not. We did not bear any malice to those that could; we just envied their good fortune. Woolworth's was, of course, a 'must' for every shopper. It was always packed and did a roaring trade. You could buy a strong, brown-paper carrier bag for a penny, and mother usually required two for her needs. She always bought one or more bags of sweets, at two pence a quarter pound and, leaving Woolworth's, we crossed the street to the Strand Cinema. My mother had previously worked there, so she knew all the staff - people such as Milly Black, who worked the ticket machine, and Edith Dugdale who was the upstairs usherette. There was a lift in the foyer, operated by a smart young chap who wore a blue uniform, complete with pillbox hat and white gloves. All of them were liberally supplied with sweets, after which we occupied free seats in the balcony.

Although I knew that I could have got in free at any time, there was only one occasion when I actually did it. It was to see a film called The Bride of Frankenstein. As it was a horror film, unaccompanied children were not admitted, and as I wished to do just that, it was necessary to use my privileged position with the staff. It was wintertime, pouring with rain and blowing hard as I made my way down Drumgold Street. Suddenly, and completely without warning, a roof slate crashed to the ground, immediately in front of my feet. Roof slates are about ten inches wide and eighteen inches long, quite thin, and with worn, jagged edges. In short, if I had been a split second earlier, it would have crashed onto either my head or shoulders, almost certainly injuring or even killing me. Was this an omen? I was already apprehensive about the film. However, undaunted I pressed on to the Strand. There was no problem about being admitted, but Edith Dugdale was concerned that I would be afraid of the film. She made me promise to leave if I was scared. In the event, I was terrified. Boris Karloff, the Monster, was not getting on very well with the female created for him by Doctor Frankenstein, so he went on the rampage. How I wished that the film would end, so that I could leave with dignity. My pride would not let me leave before the end, so I gritted my teeth and stuck it out. I still recall the scene where the Monster is trapped in a burning windmill, fighting for his life. Burning timbers crashed around him and the floodwater was getting higher all the time. Finally, it ended. Edith said that she was surprised that I had seen it through, but I assured her that I had not been in the least afraid - probably still trembling as I spoke. That night, my father's usual excellent psychological appreciation deserted him, for as I was going to bed he said, 'Mind the Monster doesn't get you in the dark.' This was the last thing that I wanted to hear and, for the first time that I can remember, I slept with the bedroom light on all night.

All the theatres and cinemas had their own electricity generators. The diesel generators for the Strand and the Picture House were situated at the top of the passageway that ran between the buildings. The Regal, Gaiety Theatre and Crescent Cinema each had its own large oil engine and belt drive to the generator. I wonder where these magnificent machines are now? Broken up for scrap years ago, I expect. Mention of the Gaiety reminds me that in the summer there was always a spectacular show there. One year there was an ice skating show, and it was thrilling to stand at the open stage door and watch the delightful chorus girls parading from the stage to their dressing rooms. The sound of the orchestra could be heard, mingling with the thump-thump of the oil engine exhaust.

Reverting to the cinema, I recall that, although many of the films were just routine action movies, there were also lots of very good historical films. There were, for example, such exciting stories as Mutiny on the Bounty (the real mutiny, of course, had a significant Manx connection); The Private Lives of Henry VIII; Emile Zola; Doctor Erlich's Magic Bullets (this about the discovery of a cure for syphilis), and many others. We probably learned as much about history from the cinema as we did at school.

CHAPTER FIVE

CHARITIES PLUS BENEFACTORS

Cold as a frog on an ice-bound pool,
Cold as the nose on an Eskimo's mule,
Cold as charity, and that's very chilly.
But not as cold as our poor Willie.
He's dead, God rest his soul.

Anon.

There were various charities in Douglas, and on the Island generally. Whether or not they deserved the epithet 'cold as charity', I can not say, as my parents never had occasion to use any of them, as far as I know. In fact, after the Second World War, my father served as a member of one, The Board of Guardians. However, if charitable bodies and benefactors are to be considered, then at the top of the list must surely be Mr. Henry Bloom Noble and the Noble Trust, because his munificence was available, not just to the poor of the town, but to everyone. Anything that has 'Noble' in its name should remind us of him. We had Noble's Hospital; Noble's Park; Noble's Baths, as well as Noble's Hall where the children had their free dinners. Some of the places have gone now, but they all provided a significant addition to the town. He also gave the earlier hospital to the town, now part of the Manx Museum. The Noble's Trustees later provided the larger and better-equipped hospital in Westmoreland Road. The Villa Marina and gardens occupy about eight acres, and is on the site of Mr. Noble's house and gardens. Douglas Corporation bought the site for £60,000. However, the Noble's trustees gave a grant of £20,000 toward the cost of the Hall and the laying-out of the grounds. The Sefton Hotel now stands on what was part of the gardens. The generosity of Mr. Noble and the Trust has, therefore, been a boon to all.

There were also other charities of a more conventional kind. For example, the 'soup kitchen' was one such. It was located near Myrtle Street, and provided a hot mid-day meal for the poor of the town. The recipients had to bring along a suitable container in which to take the food home.

The Poor Law Guardians (later The Board of Guardians) dispensed various services, including the issue to 'the deserving poor' (I do not know how poor you had to be, to be classed as 'deserving') with vouchers. These could be exchanged in selected shops for food, clothing and other necessities. The offices were located in Kingswood Grove. It was also from here that admissions to the Braddan Infirmary were administered.

Another generous benefactor was Sir John Stenhouse Goldie-Taubman, who presented the greater part of Douglas Head to the people of the town in 1870. The Goldie-Taubman family seat was The Nunnery. This magnificent house stands in very extensive grounds, and from my bedroom window - I had a good panoramic view of the whole estate. Each evening at twilight I heard the distinctive cries of the Nunnery peacocks.

The Police Treat for children was held near Christmas time. This was a very special occasion, and we all looked forward to it very much indeed. I suppose it was really intended for poor children, but in reality, every child who had a ticket was welcome. Because of the name, I suppose it was mainly the policemen (there were no woman officers) who collected the money for the event, or at least did the organising. Anyway, on the appointed day a long queue of children formed outside Noble's Hall for the free tickets. Having a ticket gave admission to the hall the following Saturday at about twelve o'clock. The hall had trestle tables and wooden benches across the width of the room, except for a passageway down the middle. The Hillside Avenue 'gang' went together, as did the children from other areas. Once inside the hall we scrambled to get a table where we could all sit together. At each place there was a bottle of pop (mineral water), supplied by, I think, the Mona Aerated Water Company. The bottle was sealed with a glass marble, and it was opened by pushing the marble into a container formed by the neck of the bottle. Nowadays you only see this type of bottle in antique shops. Meanwhile, the delicious smell of the enormous dishes of hotpot, ready to be served, was sheer heaven. I can still smell it after all those years. Once we were all seated, the host of lady helpers served everyone with a large plate of mouth-watering food. I expect the lady helpers were wives of the police officers, although I can not be sure. The hotpot was even as good as my mother could make. It was a celebration for us, so the noise was deafening. There was no fighting, and no one wasted the food.

    None of the many people who contributed to the wonderful meal was ever thanked, as far as I know, by any of the children. However, they must have realised how grateful we were - at least I hope so. After we had eaten, we were all shepherded to the cinema, usually the Royalty in Walpole Avenue. If you were lucky, your group would be seated in the balcony, somewhere that you could never aspire to normally, as it cost so much. Seats in the rear balcony cost 1/- (6p), and the best seats in the house, those in the front balcony, 1/3d (7p). The place was packed with children, and the movie was always one guaranteed to please us, such as a cowboy film. Finally, at about four o'clock, it was all over. We left in a noisy but orderly crowd, usually talking excitedly about the film. However, this wonderful day was not quite over, for on the way out we each received a bag containing an orange, an apple and a bag of boiled sweets. So we made our way home, full, happy and at peace with the world. When I look back, it is clear that a large number of firms and people must have contributed to this superb occasion besides the police, but we never knew who they were, and it never occurred to us to ask. This wonderful event continued until 1970.

Although not a charity in the accepted sense, the Douglas Gas Company was an unofficial one. Restricting the air supply to burning coal makes town gas. The result is that gas is given off and collected in the huge gasometers. Meanwhile, the burnt coal was reduced to coke, regarded as something of a waste product. The coke burned well, but was difficult to light and keep going in a domestic grate, so the Gas Company either gave it away, or charged only a nominal sum for it - I can not remember which. Consequently, it was a common sight to see someone pushing a wheelbarrow, a bogie (a box on old pram wheels) or an old pram loaded with coke. You could even have it delivered, but you had to pay a delivery charge. A huge steam driven lorry was used for this purpose, and it was kept in immaculate condition. The gas works was situated on the South Quay, near the Trafalgar Inn, and the showrooms were at the top of Victoria Street. Understandably, the lighting and heating was by gas. As it was a showcase, care was taken to ensure that the place was cosy and warm, and the lighting was quite as good as that by electricity. The window displays were always quite special with, say, a large Hornby railway layout, or a complicated Meccano construction. One in particular that I remember was a three-foot high model of the Blackpool Tower. At that time, the gas industry was a serious rival to electricity, as there was a considerable lighting and cooking load. Next door to the showroom stood a large, high class furnishing store, called Cubbon and Bregazzi's. These days they have a shop at St. Johns.

The Mayor's Fund was a charity of which I had little knowledge. It was, and to a large extent still is, a mystery to me how it worked, but basically it went something like this: Mr. Crookall was the Mayor of Douglas at one time, and he set up the fund. He arranged the purchase of a hundred or so undressed dolls, all of good quality. Lady volunteers undertook to dress them and, a little before Christmas, the dolls were put on display at the Villa Marina. Each woman had her name attached to the doll that she had dressed, so the competition was intense. One can imagine the varied and wonderful assortment of dolls that were on display. Meanwhile, by some magic process, the names of girls who were poor had been selected to receive one of the beautiful dolls. Boys, on the other hand, received a book, so clearly the girls got the better of it, thanks to the masterstroke of involving the volunteer ladies. My wife has told me that, when a little girl, she longed to have one of the dolls, but she never qualified. The nearest that she ever got was to receive a book called Hereward the Wake, that some boy had failed to collect.

The Dorcas Society was set up to give practical help to the poor. They supplied material, such as flannelette, which could be made into underwear and nighties. Another was the Coal Fund. This was operated from the Rechabite Hall in Allan Street. As usual, the poor were on the receiving end, this time entitling them to receive a hundredweight (50kg) of coal each month during the winter period.

A charity, of which I have little knowledge, is that bequeathed by Pierre Henri Josef Baume, who died in 1875. He was a Frenchman who lived in Douglas for many years, apparently in abject poverty. When he died his clothes were sold for thirteen pence (6.5p). One can imagine the surprise, then, when his will was read! He had bequeathed property to the value of more than £50,000 to certain men, with a request that the money be used for educational and other such purposes on the Island. The only thing that I knew about the fund came from George Broad. He was a musician, and I often heard him refer to the Baume scholarship which, I presume, was intended for the study of music.

The Work Scheme for the unemployed operated from the beginning of November until the end of March. As the name suggests, it provided work through the winter months, but only for men. The work was very hard, as it was all manual labouring. The workers travelled in open lorries, and the work often consisted of digging ditches or working in quarries. Other projects were just as hard, but at least provided a lasting testimonial to their efforts. For example, they constructed the sunken gardens on the promenade, and Summer Hill Glen. Mention of the promenade reminds me that at one time the sea wall used to be close to Strand Street. A small section of the wall can be seen along the lane behind Strand Street, looking from Howard Street. The new sea wall was built during the Governorship of Lord Loch, and accommodates the Loch Promenade. It was completed in 1878.

Before the war, it was relatively common to see both children and adults who suffered from various bone diseases, such as rickets, knock- knees and other deformities. It was to help unfortunate people such as these, that a charity, of which I know very little, was formed. It was called the Cripples Guild, and it had a medical basis. Who ran it, and from where, I can not say. Some of the bone deficiencies were dietary in origin, and one of the things dispensed by the charity was called Radio Malt. I do not know if there was any difference between it and ordinary malt, but I suppose there must have been. Anyway, it must have been a comfort to the sufferers of the various diseases that someone was trying to help them. I remember John Kelly, who lived in the avenue, suffered from rickets, but he was an adult, so I expect it was too late for him to cure the ailment.

An interesting person, but one that I never saw, was Mr. Colby Cubbon. He was reputed to be a millionaire; at any rate, he was undoubtedly wealthy. He owned a steam yacht called the Glen Strathallan, which seemed to spend most of its time moored near E B Christian's garage on the North Quay. I expect he sailed in it often, but my recollection is of it usually being tied-up. A wooden full-rigged ship, which sailed from Norway, was often moored nearby. It carried timber for Quiggin's yard. However, back to Colby Cubbon. He was, I understand, a keen radio ham, and he played a significant part in the marine life of the town. He presented three lifeboats to the RNLI, the Douglas lifeboat, 'Colby Cubbon No. 1', being launched on 25th July, 1956.

Probably there were other benefactors and charities operating at this time, but I can not bring them to mind. In any case, the main point is that there was a strong social conscience amongst the better-off people to do what they could to help those in need. Living conditions for the poor must have been hard indeed, and the various charities could not alter that, but at least it made life a little more bearable for them.

CHAPTER SIX

INTERESTING PEOPLE

If you have to tell them who you are, you aren't anybody.

Gregory Peck.

There were a number of personalities in Douglas. One was Harry Winter. He owned a shop, and also sold vegetables from a flat-cart, which was pulled by a donkey. He drove the cart along Hillside Avenue, bawling as he went some sales pitch that had become unrecognisable as English, from too-frequent use. Harry's donkey was something of a film star, as it had featured prominently in No Limit. We used to shriek with laughter at the oft-told joke that went:

'Why is Harry Winter the cleverest man in Douglas?'
'Because he is the only one who can go into a pub for a drink and leave his ass outside.'

Another character was called Billy Corrin. He was a large man, but had lost his left arm below the elbow, presumably in the war. He must have been a very strong chap, as he pushed a heavy, wooden ice cream cart all over Douglas. When he came to the avenue, he stopped outside number twelve. There were no calls or musical jingles - you just knew that he was there. If I could persuade my mother to part with a halfpenny, I would rush along the avenue to buy a small cone. A large one cost a penny, and for two pence, you could buy a wafer. This was a thick layer of ice cream between two wafer biscuits. You never see wafers now, only cones. How Billy managed to push that heavy cart up those steep hills, when he only had one good arm, is a mystery to me. He was a common sight all over town, and a favourite spot, of course, was on the promenade. I expect he did a roaring business.

We had two organ grinders. One organ was quite a large affair, mounted on two wheels and pulled by a skinny pony. The man wore a cloth cap, and was quite a surly fellow. Usually a young boy, probably his son, was with him. The grinder looked bored as he turned the handle of the hurdy-gurdy, but the music was lively and included the popular songs of the day. I remember that he collected the coppers in a tambourine, although I can not recall him ever saying 'Thank you.' I expect that he must have done, really. It is just that I can not recall it.

The other organ grinder was Felario. His was a much smaller affair, which he carried from place to place. The organ was contained in a box about two feet square, and when in use it rested on a single wooden leg. He had a monkey, as was expected of any self-respecting grinder, and he was a fine, be-whiskered chap. He looked, and probably was, of Italian extraction. Both the grinders brought a little happiness and cheer to the area, and it says something for the people in the avenue that they contributed enough from their meagre cash to make it worthwhile for them to come from time to time.

Outside the Villa Marina entrance, there was always a man selling carnations. He would be there in the morning, afternoon and, most important of all, in the early evening. In those days, being casually dressed amounted to little more than wearing your navy-blue suit with the collar of your white shirt open. If you were going to the theatre or to a dance, then everyone was smartly dressed. The men wore lounge suit, collar and tie, and the ladies, crisp summer dresses. There was, therefore, a great demand for the beautifully prepared flowers, either as a buttonhole for the men, or pinned to the dress of the women. Looking smart and elegant was *de rigueur* in those days. How different to now, when many young people seem to go out of their way to look as casual as possible. The flower seller had a large wicker basket, of the type used by errand boys. It had a baize inset, on which the various coloured flowers were displayed, each with its stem neatly bound in silver paper. I think a bloom cost six pence, so was quite expensive. But it certainly seemed to me to be a lovely way for a young man to impress his girlfriend.

There were several boot black's, one of whom had his pitch outside the Mona Bouquet shop at Greensill's corner. He had a small Cherry Blossom box with his gear in, and on the top was a little platform for the customer to rest his foot. The bootblack knelt on the ground and polished the leather until it had a brilliant shine. I do not know how much a shoe- shine cost, but I think it would be about three pence.

The people that I have mentioned worked in the summer. However, on a less happy note, there was one unfortunate man who walked down the avenue each day at five o'clock. He was over six feet tall, and always wore a navy-blue suit. His head shook continuously, vigorously and uncontrollably. The story was that the poor man had been shell shocked during the war, but I never knew whether this was true. We never knew where he came from or where he went. We never spoke to him or he to us.

The truth was that we were embarrassed by his sad condition, and never made fun of him.

The fish cart was pulled by a pony, and came along the avenue about once a week. The driver would yell, "Fresh herring, Peel herring" except that it sounded like "Frer hen. Peel hen" from over-use. On the flat-cart was a good selection of cheap fish, all exposed to the weather. There were several other flat-cart people, such as Messers Skillen and Lowther, who had hawker's licences. Each of them had a boy in my class at school, and they lived in old Douglas. Old Douglas was the area consisting of the North and South Quays and the part where the bus station now stands. That particular part of the town was demolished in 1936, and a large car park was built in its place. I can not imagine why, though, as parking was not a problem as far as I can remember. After the Second World War the present bus station was built on the site.

A well-known newspaper seller was called Johnny Puttynose. The Green Final was a four-page paper printed on the Examiner press each Saturday evening. Its main function was to list that day's classified football results, and it hit the streets at about six o'clock. The paper was in great demand, as it provided the early means of checking if this was to be your turn to scoop the pools. In those days, the football pools were a greater draw than even the National Lottery is today. Incidentally, my mother's cousin was married to John Moores, the founder of Littlewoods Pools. Mother and Ruby corresponded regularly, although that did not help us to win the pools, of course. Anyway, Johnny Puttynose would stand on the street corner bawling, 'Green Final' but, like the fish man, constant use had changed it almost out of recognition to 'Een Fineel'. The football results were given on the wireless at five-thirty on Saturday, and dad assiduously copied them down. It was the one time that everyone was obliged to keep quiet. As soon as he had completed copying the results he gave me a penny and told me to go and get the Green Final, hot off the press. I could never understand why he needed a confirmation that yet again we had failed to win the pools. However, dutifully off I went to get the paper from Johnny.

During the summer, the sea-wall side of the promenade was usually lined with charabancs (coaches). Each vehicle had a blackboard propped against the front wheel advertising the next trip to places such as Glen Helen, Port St. Mary, Laxey Glen Gardens, Mystery Tour and so on. Meanwhile, the unfortunate visitors who happened to walk past were subjected to a sustained harangue from the driver-cum-touts to sign up for their particular trip. They were nuisances, and eventually the law forbade touting. The number and variety of the charabancs was amazing. Every one was beautifully painted, and had such charming names as Happy Days, Pride of Mona, Happy Go Lucky, Lady Isabella and many others. Certainly in the summertime, Douglas was a vibrant place, full of life and colour. It was a wonderful place in which to grow up.

From time to time, there was a parade of the Orangemen. They marched in grand style along the promenade, headed by flag bearers and men who marched with a military gait, wore bowler hats and many of whom had a beautifully coloured sash draped across his chest. The parades were a stirring sight, particularly as there was always one or more bands playing. I must confess that I never really had much idea about what the Orangemen were.

Another impressive sight was the Salvation Army band leading the way along the promenade to the area of beach opposite the Palace. There they held a service, which was usually well attended by visitors. Upon completion, they re-formed and marched away in grand style, the band playing, flag borne on high and the women executing intricate patterns in the air with their tambourines. There was another religious group called the Church Army, who held beach services. These, too, were well attended, but instead of the flamboyance of the Salvation Army, there would only be one or two speakers.

The scissors-sharpener's "shop". It provided a regular service in Hillside Avenue between the wars. It is now in the Manx Museum. (Courtesy Manx Heritage)

About once a year, the scissors-grinder appeared in the avenue. He had a purpose-built, wooden, box-like contraption with a single large wheel. The whole rig was painted dark brown, and can now be seen in the Manx Museum. The operator pushed the rig along on its wheel, but when he set up his pitch, the assembly rested on legs. A belt was slipped over the wheel and this drove the grindstones, whilst the operator pedalled away. He could put a razor edge on tools ranging from scissors, knives, hatchets, garden shears - pretty much anything.

Occasionally, towards the end of the summer, the French-onion man came around. He looked like the characters portrayed in the cartoons, riding his bicycle with bundles of onions hung around his neck and over the handles of his bicycle. He wore a beret, which was a very French thing to do in those days. Onions were so cheap that I can not see how he could possibly have made a living selling them, but he must have done so, as he kept coming back.

Before the war and immediately afterward, no holiday resort was worth its salt if it did not have a visit from Lobby Ludd. This was a very good way of increasing the circulation of one of the newspapers, the Daily Despatch, I think. It was announced in the paper that he would be on, say, Douglas promenade between specified hours on a particular day. The paper showed a tantalising view of him in head and shoulders three-quarter view from the rear. This revealed very little, except that he wore a trilby hat, so you had no real idea of what he looked like. If you thought that you had spotted him, you had to approach him with a set form of words. These went along the lines of, 'You are Lobby Ludd, and I claim the prize.' You also had to be carrying a copy of the latest issue of the paper. I think the prize was a pound note, so it was well worth winning.

Killip's was a tea blender's shop, which stood in Ridgeway Street. It was an exotic place, with containers from all over the world, stamped with the names of places such as Darjeeling, Assam, Ceylon,

China and many more. Customers could ask for any combination of tea, and Mr. Killip would blend it expertly. Next door, there was a seed merchant's shop. Sacks of seed stood on the wooden floor, and it had a nice 'agricultural' smell. You will have gathered that there was very little pre-packaging at that time, presumably because labour was so cheap that do-it-yourself service by the assistants was economic. It also meant that the customers had friendly and personal service. There was the additional advantage for more wealthy customers that they had real choice, such as having their tea blended at Killip's.

Once every five years we had a visit from the King of the Road, the huge steamroller used in conjunction with the tar sprayer to re-surface the avenue. We would stand well back and watch in awe as the mighty roller clanked back and forth, pressing the gravel chippings into the freshly laid tar. The smell was very special, being an enchanting blend of hot oil from the engine and molten tar. How we longed to be allowed to ride on the roller, but we never dared to ask. The drivers never spoke to us, let alone invite us to climb aboard. When work finished for the day, the roller was left unattended, but even then, we resisted the urge to climb on to it. The machine used for melting the cakes of asphalt was also left unattended, but in this case we had no desire to board it, as it was filthy.

Following the tragic death of Mr. Johnson, the family left the avenue, and was replaced by the Readshaws. Mr. Readsaw operated a string of rowing boats from the promenade steps. One of his daughter's, Gladys, played the accordion, and on summer evenings older children taught us dances, such as the Palais Glide, the waltz and Underneath the Spreading Chestnut Tree, whilst she provided the music. The dancing was done near the street lamp, outside long-suffering Mrs. Cain's house, number twenty-four. Gladys became a senior nurse at Noble's Hospital and remained there, as far as I know, until she retired.

In my class at school, there was a particularly unassuming boy. He was always neatly dressed, and was usually somewhere in the middle of the class at exam time. After leaving school, I lost contact with him, until one day in 1947, when I casually met up with him again. I asked him how he was going on, and I was staggered when he replied, quite nonchalantly, 'I've just come out of clink.' It seems that he had been in prison in England for some high-level thieving. I suppose the moral is that you can not tell what your classmates will turn out like. Often it will be entirely different to anything that you could imagine.

Noble's Park was always referred to as the Rec., and the groundsman was a fearsome fellow called Mr.Snell. He ruled his kingdom with a rod of iron. He was not a very big man, but he had plenty of 'presence'. I only remember him wearing one outfit, consisting of a tweed jacket; boots and his trousers tucked into leather gaiters. He looked every inch a gamekeeper. If you dared to walk on any of the grassed areas that sported a 'keep off' sign, he would appear from nowhere and yell from yards away to keep off the grass. I never saw him smile, nor did he ever have a companion. He was probably content with his own company, and he certainly intimidated us children.

Two boys who lived on the North Quay were regular visitors to the avenue. They usually came in the early evening, pushing a bogey full of chopped and bundled firewood for sale. They were nice lads, and we would always chat to them, but they never accepted our invitation to stay and play for a while. I suppose they wanted to get on with the round. I expect since getting home from school, they had collected, chopped and bundled the firewood that they were now selling. To them, we must have appeared as drones.

Mr. Jolly lived in the avenue, in a house called Jollity Cottage, and he was the door-man at the Strand Cinema. He, like most of the door-men, had a magnificent brown uniform. It had lots of gold braid, and he looked splendid. He stood at the entrance to the cinema, informing everyone in a loud voice that there was standing room only in the rear stalls, that the front stalls were full and other, similar, information. I must say, I never quite understood why these people were needed, as we could easily have found the information for ourselves. On the other hand, it provided a job, as well as making the cinema a little more 'posh'. The other Douglas Cinemas, the Regal, Picture House and the Royalty, also each had a door-man, so the positions created four welcome jobs.

One of the characters in the avenue was a chap called Tommy Shropshire. He was a couple of years older than me, and used to do some hair-brained things. One that I particularly admired him for was his trick-cycling act. He would ride his cycle down the hill from Westmoreland Road to get up speed. Then he would put his feet on the handlebars and hold his arms outstretched, so steering the machine with his feet. He was going quite fast as he did this, and a part of the act was to see how close to the railings at the bottom of the avenue that he could get before having to brake. An alternative trick was to stand on the saddle and hold the handlebars whilst he rode down the hill. These tricks were never done for an audience; he just performed them as and when he felt like it. For example, we would be playing a game in the street, when suddenly Tommy would come flying past with his arms outstretched. There were several members of the Shropshire family, and one of Tommy's older sisters was called Elsie. She married, and had a daughter called Audrey, who is now my sister-in-law. It's a small world!

Mr. Cunningham, of Cunningham's Holiday Camp, was rather special to me. This was not because of the camp, but because he actually owned and flew his own aeroplane. It was a small, high-wing monoplane; it was painted blue, and could probably carry two or three passengers. He flew it from the grassed field owned by him, just beyond the Rec. When the aircraft was stationary, we would gather round to admire it and look inside, but no one touched it or interfered with it in any way. We felt that Mr. Cunningham must have been a good pilot by just being able to get the machine off the ground and then to be able to land it again. Later, when we were in the Air Training Corps, he gave us some talks about the art of flying.

Well, there it is, - a small selection of the interesting people I knew of. Clearly, there were many more that I have forgotten, and others whom I did not even know. In his way, each added something to the life of the town. Strangely, I can not recall any similar women. There must have been some, and I expect I will remember them when it is too late for inclusion in the book.

CHAPTER SEVEN

WORK

Only fools and horses work.

My very first job was at Hinton's Nursery Gardens in Brunswick Road. As I was only thirteen, I could only work for half a day at a time by law. Therefore, I worked in the afternoon during the summer holidays until six o'clock. The work involved picking fruit, such as loganberries, raspberries and gooseberries. For this, I received the princely sum of about nine pence a week. After I finished work at Hinton's, I dashed home, had my tea and changed clothes for my second job. This was selling programmes at the Crescent Pavilion. It was a small, single storey, wooden structure. It stood next to the Crescent Cinema. Opulent and luxurious were not words that came readily to mind when you entered the place. In fact, if it rained hard, someone in the audience would be sure to raise an umbrella amidst howls of laughter. No one ever complained, as far as I know. The programmes cost a penny each, and I was paid a penny for every dozen sold. Obviously, with such a dilapidated building, there were hardly any people in the audience if the weather was good, so I would not even earn a penny. On the other hand, if it rained the place would be full, and I could earn as much as sixpence. I enjoyed the show, and my favourite in the cast was a beautiful soubrette called Zoe Wheeler. I was thrilled if I saw her outside and she said 'Hello'. Norman Langford was the star of the show.

I enjoyed walking along the promenade to the pavilion. Once, early in the summer of 1939, the walk was particularly exciting, as HMS Royal Oak was lying at anchor in the bay. She was a capital ship with fifteen-inch guns, and rode at anchor at the Onchan Head end of the bay. She was the first battleship that I had ever seen, and I was duly impressed by its huge size. She was on a courtesy visit, and remained at anchor for several days. Then it was gone. Gone for ever, in the event, as this magnificent vessel was torpedoed and sunk at her anchorage at Scapa Flow on October 14th, with the loss of 833 lives. The news of the loss was a great blow to me, as I could not visualise how it was possible. However, as I walked along the promenade all this was in the future. As far as I was concerned at the time, this magnificent ship had merely sailed away to some other bay to be admired by another set of people.

Another, but less welcome, vessel that anchored in the bay later that summer, was a German 'Strength Through Joy' holiday liner. It seems that if you worked particularly hard for Germany, you could qualify for a holiday on this vessel; but I was not at all pleased to see this 'enemy' ship enjoying Manx hospitality. The newsreels at the time were full of scenes of aggressive, marching German soldiers, and huge military rallies in support of Hitler, which caused me some disquiet. The Territorial Army soldiers from the camp at Onchan Head were a happy crowd, but how could they match the arrogant Germans? Of course, I never doubted that they could, but I failed to work out how it was so.

One good thing about working at the Crescent Pavilion was that it gave me free admission to the cinema next door. I took full advantage of this, and saw a different film each week. Some that I recall include Roberta, Roman Scandals, Bulldog Jack, East Side of Heaven and various others.

Shortly after my fourteenth birthday, I left school and, for the first time, had to find a proper job. Or, rather, the first job that I could find. This turned out to be as a messenger boy for Cannell's Café in Duke Street. The bakery was in the basement, the shop and a café on the ground floor, and a further café on the second floor. The food made in the bakery was superb, although the place was quite dilapidated. There was a brisk demand for the cakes and bread to be delivered, and that was where I came in. Unfortunately, Cannell's did not have a carrier bicycle, so I was obliged to walk all over Douglas with a large delivery basket on my arm. Sometimes it would be to Queen's Promenade, at others to Ballanard Road. Quickly, though, I became friendly with the messenger boys from the shops nearby, so soon I was delivering my goods on a Maypole cycle one day, Clucas' flower shop another, and Lipton's another and so on. I would just take any cycle that I came across. The other boys knew about this, but they did not seem to have any objection. In fact, we were all good pals.

Next to the Maypole, there was one of Gore's rock shops. There was usually a crowd of visitors watching, through the window, how the rock was made. It is not commonly realised that the art of getting the letters into the sticks of rock was developed in the Isle of Man. However, my days at Canell's Café were not very happy. I hated the boredom and lack of purpose about the job. Whenever I had the chance, I would slip away to the bakery to help. Three men and two women worked there. The oldest man was passed retirement age, but it was educational to watch him work. When icing, say, a wedding cake, he could produce the most intricate patterns and beautiful lettering, without any plans or guides, just out of his head. Later on, when war had been declared, he was the only person that I knew who said that he was not sure that we would win. Maybe he was more honest with himself than the rest of us. Reg Hannay, who was much younger, was furious with him, and would tell him to shut up. I liked Reg because he was always cheerful with me. I would punch out meat pie and jam tart cases for him, and help in any other way that I could. On one occasion, he told me to put vanilla essence into a large jar of cream that was being prepared. I selected the essence from the battery of dough-stained bottles, and poured a good amount into the cream. Immediately, I realised that it was not vanilla, but lemon essence. I rushed to tell Reg, who just laughed as he scooped a handful of cream from the jar where I had poured the essence. He said, 'Put lots of vanilla in and no one will be the wiser.' The third man in the bakery was about twenty. He was called Doug Hughes, and had been the messenger before me. He lived in Pulrose, and was always cheerful. He would tell me about the dances he went to at the Palais and about his romance. When we had some spare time, he taught me to dance the Foxtrot, Quickstep, Slow Foxtrot and Waltz. Soon he was called-up for military service and, as far as I know, was killed on his twenty-first birthday, whilst serving in North Africa. The two ladies in the bakery were Florrie and Doreen. Later, a young, good-looking girl, called Doris joined them. I do not remember much about them, as they always seemed to be just getting on with the job.

One of my jobs was to clean the upstairs café windows. This necessitated me sitting on the signboard with my back to Duke Street. I took as long as possible as it was so pleasant to watch the visitors who thronged the street below, and to listen to the music which came from the milk bar opposite. The popular music of the day was played on a radiogram, South of the Border, sung by Bing Crosby, being my favourite. The weather was beautiful during that halcyon period just before war was declared, and the people appeared to be happy and carefree. I think my pay was about three shillings a week. Probably that was too much, as I hated the job and must have been the worst errand boy that ever worked there. Compared to Doug Hughes I must have been a non-starter. On Saturday's the number of deliveries was too much for me on my own, so the Manageress, Miss Kermode, had an arrangement with a farmer called Eddie Cooile to drive me around in his van. Often, though, we would get back to the cafÈ, only to find that there was still a box of cakes, or a loaf of bread in the van. How I prayed that I could get away from that awful job. However, the months crept by and still I was stuck with it - June, July, and August. Surely, it would end soon?

All the talk at this time was of war. The shameful Munich agreement of 1938 seemed to have had no effect at all on Hitler's ambitions. I was fourteen at the time, so I am not in a position to say with any authority how the people felt. Probably there was much foreboding, particularly amongst those old enough to recall the horrors of the Great War. After all, it was only twenty years since that war had ended. However, the impression that I gained was of people who, deep down felt that war was inevitable. They were doubtless saddened by the prospect, but not in any way downhearted. The carefree gaiety of the visitors seemed just the same as ever, and I often wonder how many of those happy young people were soon, like Doug Hughes, to die. To people of my age, of course, the prospect of war thrilled us with excitement. To us it was going to be a great adventure. In our defence, I suppose that it can be said that we were very young - and naive

One evening in August 1939, I was on the sea front at the Queen's Promenade end. It was about nine o'clock and the very first practice blackout took place. The lovely illuminations were suddenly extinguished, plunging the whole promenade into darkness. A crowd of young men and women quickly gathered, all laughing and holding lighted matches aloft. The leader of the group was saying things like:
"What will we do with Hitler?"
"String him up."
So it went on. A good lark, and in its way quite touching. From a café nearby, the record of the Benny Goodman orchestra playing 'And The Angels Sing', floated on the breeze. That song will always remind me of the outbreak of the war.

A common feeling at the time was that when the war came there would immediately be wave after wave of German bombers devastating the whole country. Many of the newsreels had shown how easily the cities and towns of Spain were reduced to rubble in the Civil War. The other fear was that gas bombs would be dropped. The Government understood this, for they arranged for everyone, including babies, to be issued with a gas mask. In the event, no such bombs were used, a tribute, we thought, to Hitler's humanitarianism. In fact, it turned out that documents captured after the war indicated that the Germans would certainly have used gas, had they not been led to believe that British retaliation would have been swift and much worse. In fact, it seems that we had no gas bombs at all, so this piece of disinformation which was leaked to the enemy was most successful, for which we should all be grateful.

In 1939, there was an ominous happening. The Germans had entered teams for the TT Races for several years, but had never been able to stop the all-conquering Norton team from their regular first, second and third places in the Senior race. The Germans had teams such as DKW, NSU and BMW, but what the letters stood for was a mystery. I do not think there was any animosity towards the teams, particularly as they were about to be routinely beaten by the Norton team again. But it was not to be. For the first time ever, a foreign machine (and German at that) won the Senior TT. We were stunned. How was such a thing possible? The winner was called Georg Meier, and when he returned to Germany the beautiful trophy (a statue of Mercury, the God of speed) went with him. Probably this would be the last that we would ever see of it. It would be melted down for the silver it contained. Courageously, Herr Meier kept the trophy safe until the war was over, after which he returned it without any fuss. Nevertheless, in 1939 our world was turned upside down by the German win. Could it be an augury of things to come? Maybe they were better than we thought? None of this altered the basic feeling that we would win, but now it may take a little longer.

I continued to work at Cannell's until March 1940, when thankfully I got a job as an apprentice electrician at Lawton's in John Street. My pay was five shillings (25p) a week. It was a welcome change to work with tools, instead of delivering cakes. The electricians were a good crowd, such as Harold Brantwood, Frank Openshaw, Alf Slater (who operated the Ghost Train before the war) and Billy Wade. There were three apprentices, including me. The firm was kept very busy on war work. I was usually with Frank Openshaw, installing tubular electric heaters in the main rooms of the houses in the Palace Internment Camp, which consisted of the houses on the Onchan side of the Palace. Almost all the promenade houses, and many others as well, were commandeered for war use. The OCTU (Officer Cadet Training Unit) occupied the Villiers Hotel; the Loch Promenade houses became HMS Valkyrie; the Empress Promenade ones were used by the RAF Regiment and the Alexander, Waverley, Duckworth's and the Metropole Hotel formed the Metropole Internment Camp. I also worked for a short time installing electric lighting in a huge refrigerated food depot in a quarry, somewhere near Summer Hill. It was such a massive installation that I expect it is still there. However, as I said earlier, I worked mainly in the Palace Camp, and this included houses such as Friendship; Dominion; Edelweiss; Good Companions and Beresford. The internees were known as 18b's, as that was the Regulation under which they were detained. They were Italian civilians plus merchant seamen who had been in the UK at the outbreak of war. They were treated well but, understandably, resented being interned. Many of them could not even speak Italian, so classes in that language were popular. There were quite a few well-known people there, such as Mario Zampi, a famous film director, and the Director of the Lancia-Fiat Company. I found the internees quiet and well behaved, although in his book Paper Hero, about the camps, a former prisoner states that fights were common. What I did find, was that they were light-fingered. If any tools were left unattended, they would disappear. Similarly, if floorboards were lifted which revealed bundles of bell wire going to the massive indicator boards, then that, too, would go. The wire would re-appear as the rigging of a sailing ship. As far as I am aware, the missing tools, wire and so on, were not used for clandestine activities - only for quite open use in the workshops. Spaghetti was a favourite part of their diet, as you may well imagine, and in the kitchens the pull-up clothes drying racks, which were suspended from the ceiling, were usually festooned with the stuff. They clearly had enough food, as both Frank and I were regularly invited to stay for lunch with them, and often we accepted.

However, one thing that they certainly did not have enough of was female company, this being an all-male camp. The married internees were permitted a visit by their wives every so often, and that was that. Frank was married to particularly glamorous lady called Lil and, rather naughtily, he would get her to walk tantalisingly slowly along the promenade in front of the camp, causing considerable and predictable excitement amongst the sex-starved men.

The boss at Lawton's was called Mr. Pascoe. He was a man of ample proportions, and one to whom I was destined to be indebted. Although most of my time was spent working with Frank at the Palace Camp, I was required from time to time to work elsewhere. In 1942, for example, I was sent to help at the Ballaqueeney Hotel in Port St. Mary. It was used by the OCTU, and my work was similar to that at the Palace Camp, but overtime was required until nine o'clock each day. For this I was paid a penny (1/2p) an hour. There was no way of escaping it, as to get back to Douglas I had to travel in the firm's battered wreck of a van. This overtime business was serious for me, as by the time that I got home it was too late to go dancing. In any case, at one penny an hour it was just not worth it. I asked Mr. Pascoe to allow me to work in Douglas, but he said that it was not possible. So I asked for extra overtime pay, but he said that this was not possible either, as he was already paying the union rate. Therefore, in desperation I hatched a plan. I contacted the other two apprentices, who also objected to the overtime pay, and we agreed that each of us would hand in his notice at the same time. It was reasoned that, faced with the loss of all of his apprentices, Mr. Pascoe would agree to pay us more. Accordingly, the following Thursday was set for the day of action. I was working at the Central Hotel in Douglas at the time, and when Mr. Pascoe called to see how the work was progressing, I informed him that I was giving my notice, and would finish in a week's time. I was a little disappointed that he seemed so unconcerned but, I thought, he jolly well will be when the others do the same. It was not until the following day, Friday, that I met up with them. I excitedly asked them what Mr. Pascoe's reaction had been when they handed in their notice? To my horror, they said that they had talked it over between themselves and decided not to proceed, but they had not bothered to tell me. So there I was, the only one committed to losing his job. I made desperate enquiries with all the other likely people who could get me with their firm. One such was Mr. Hales from Hillside Avenue. He worked for the Douglas Corporation Electricity Department, and he did his best for me. However, it was no good, as during the war all firms had to reinstate all their apprentices after the conflict. They were already committed to more than they required, so could not take on any more. Remorselessly the time went on for my notice to expire. The day when I was to leave Lawton's finally arrived, and I still had no prospect of getting another job. This was the situation when I went to the office to get my last pay envelope. As I was at this time a third-year apprentice, my pay was ten shillings (50p) a week. From now on, I would have to become a labourer. Mr. Pascoe called me into the office. I thought it was just to wish me well, but this was not so. Instead, he said that, as there was plenty of work in, would I reconsider my notice for a few weeks to help him out. I lied that I had a lot of job offers, but as a favour I would do as he asked. Of course, on both sides this was one of those, 'Little does he know that I know' situations, for he knew perfectly well that I would be out of a job. He had the power to make me grovel, but he did not even make me apologise. Instead he allowed me to continue to work for him, and even gave me the excuse that I was doing him a favour. The incident was never mentioned, and I will always remember the magnanimity that he showed me. Possibly, he, deep down, respected me for my stance, but I will never know. I often wondered how I would have reacted had our roles been reversed. Not, I think, in such an understanding manner. I left Lawton's in 1943 to join the RAF, and returned to complete my apprenticeship in 1947. These days I despair when I read of so many seemingly stupid decisions made by magistrates and others in authority. If only they showed the same common sense as Mr. Pascoe, we might all have more confidence in our justice systems.

This is probably a suitable place to mention some things of interest from that time. For example, almost all shirts worn by men were of the over-the-head type. The ones that buttoned all the way down the front, known as American style, were only being introduced then. Similarly, zip fasteners were not in very much demand. They could be had as optional extras instead of buttons on the fly of trousers for gents, but buttons were normally preferred. There was no sliced bread, and sweets were often counted out. So, if I had a penny, I used to buy six Golden Charm chocolate covered sweets at the shop in Circular Road, owned by the Misses Watterson. A two ounce bar of chocolate cost two pence, and the only 'plastic type' materials were Cellophane and Bakelite. Petrol cost one shilling and eleven pence a gallon (12p), cigarettes eleven pence halfpenny for a packet of twenty (6p), and outside Billy Corrin's shop in Drumgold Street there was a cigarette machine where you could buy Plus Two's. You put a penny in the machine and received a packet containing two cigarettes and two matches. This machine was popular with us boys if we had a penny to spend, as it made a pleasant change from 'smoking' brown paper. Up to 1939 one of the Douglas Corporation buses (number thirteen, I think) had solid rubber tyres. There was a policeman on point duty during the day at the junction of Police Station Hill and the top of Victoria Street. He stood in the middle of the road and regulated the traffic easily, efficiently and with seemingly complete nonchalance. It was about 1936 that the first traffic lights appeared on the Island. They were at the corner of York Road, and were known to all as the 'Roboes', i.e., robots. At that time, we really did go there, just to stand and watch the traffic lights change. This business of mispronouncing names was commonplace, primarily due to us having little contact with foreign languages. Thus, the film Rendezvous was called Ren-dez-vus by my classmates. In a similar manner, The Last Days of Pompeii became The Last Days of Pomp-ee-I, a well-known Douglas shop called Bon Marché was referred to as Bonn March and a café was always referred to as a cafee.

Traditionally, all schoolboys wore short trousers until they left school at fourteen, except for the High School boys. It was a magic day that you first appeared in public wearing your 'longies' - you were no longer a child, but an adolescent. Almost invariably, those first long trousers were of cheap, thick, grey material, bought in Marks and Spencer's for five shillings. Once you started to wear 'longies' you stopped playing in the street with the other children, as you were considered too old for such things. In their turn, the girls stopped wearing the standard school uniform of gym-slip, white blouse and black stockings (held up by knicker-elastic garters), and wore 'grown-up' dresses and started to use make-up. Such were the outward signs that we were slipping gently away from our wonderful age of innocence.

It was a law-abiding world, and I only knew of one boy who boasted that he had stolen things. Even then, it only amounted to a few sweets, and did not involve any damage. However, one winter evening I was walking with him along Hill Street past a parked car. As was common at that time, it was unlocked. A small brown paper parcel lay on the back seat, and he calmly opened the door and stole the parcel. I pleaded with him to put it back, but he took no notice. When we got to the painter and decorators shop owned by F W Oates, which stood on the corner of Allan street and Westmoreland Road, he opened the parcel. He was disgusted to find that it contained a picture in a cardboard mount of a young girl. Disdainfully, he threw it on the ground and walked away. I picked it up and re-wrapped it as best that

I could, went back to the car and replaced it on the back seat. I refused to have any contact with the other boy again. I expect that we were about thirteen at the time.

But the honesty of most people was just taken for granted. For example, my uncle had a grocery store in Marathon Drive, and each Friday he delivered groceries to my mother in an open-topped Jowett car. The boxes of groceries awaiting delivery were piled on the back seat, there for the taking if anyone was that way inclined - but they never were. The car was left unattended for over half an hour whilst he had a cup of tea with my mother, but never once was anything stolen.

As late as 1939 there were still some bathing machines for hire on Douglas beach. They were cumbersome wooden huts, mounted on large wheels, for the use of modest bathers. I do not recall any of them being hired. Mind you, some people should have used them, as I was amazed at the contortions some bathers got into whilst dressing/undressing with a towel wrapped round their body. The beach at Douglas was quite stony, and so in 1935 groins were put in place. These simple structures had a dramatic effect. Thus, whereas before the groins there was a drop at the War Memorial to the beach of some ten feet, this quickly changed until you could just step off the promenade. In addition, the amount of sand on the beach increased substantially.

It was in 1936 that I saw my first modern tin opener. It was at the Tynwald Fair, and a salesman was demonstrating this ultra-modern kitchen gadget. I was very impressed as I watched, for he opened tins easily, cleanly and swiftly, whereas I was used to seeing my mother hacking away at the tins with one of those 'work-it-up-and-down' things. The new gadget was called a Jiffy Can Opener. Its business end was much the same as those today, but it did not have any long handles. Instead you just clamped it and held the tin itself whilst you operated the device.

When going to a function such as a dance, it was obligatory for men to wear a white shirt, the cuffs of which were held to the correct length by armbands. These were lightweight elastic loops, worn above the elbow outside the sleeves. The men had their hair plastered down with brilliantine or Brylcreem or similar stuff, whilst the ladies had hairstyles such as Marcel Waves and Pageboy. My mother wore her hair in a bun for many years. When she let her hair down to wash it, she would dry it by sitting in front of the fire, and it would reach to the floor. I still remember my sense of betrayal when I came home from school one day to find that she had cut it, so that it barely reached her shoulders.

At dances it was common for men to bring a pair of lightweight, patent leather shoes to dance in. Similarly, the ladies brought lightweight dance shoes, normally coloured gold or silver. The rituals at the dances were rigidly enforced. For example, girls never asked boys to dance, only boys could ask girls. However, when asked, a girl was quite entitled to refuse without causing any offence. Commonly, though, having refused, she was expected to sit out that dance. Unattached girls usually congregated at a particular part of the ballroom so that the boys knew which ones they could ask. It was considered very bad form to approach a girl who was escorted by her boyfriend. Each dance consisted of three tunes, after which the dancers left the floor. At the end of each dance, the band was applauded. The final tune of the evening was always the Last Waltz and desperation was setting in if you had failed to find a girl who would allow you to take her home. All the available girls would be whisked onto the dance floor, either by the lucky chaps already fixed up, or by those with fingers crossed that they, too, would be lucky. Immediately after the last dance everyone stood to attention whilst the National Anthem was played, although often a truncated version of the tune was deemed sufficient.

One of the delights of the pre-war and immediate post-war period was the amazing range of bread that was available. As already

There were several novelty vehicles in Douglas during the summer in the 1930's. This 'bottle van' was a common sight, and was one of five, some of which advertised Worthington, and the others Bass, beer. It is now in the Bass Museum.
(Courtesy of the Bass Museum, Burton upon Trent.)

stated, there was no sliced bread. On the other hand, mouth-watering fresh bread with such names as Vienna, Tin, Cottage, Sandwich, a plaited loaf whose name I can not remember, and many more were commonplace. Bakers, such as A J Winkle from Foxdale, delivered bread and cakes in the avenue from a small van. It may be that my memory is at fault, but I feel that the vanilla slices, maids of honour, marzipan squares and so on, were much larger than those today.

Lounging in deck chairs was a common sight on the beach. Often the men would be wearing the navy-blue trousers of their two-piece suit, complete with elastic braces, a white open-necked shirt with the sleeves rolled up, and a white handkerchief with the corners knotted, worn as head protection. Today the picture may seem laughable, but then it hardly warranted a second glance.

Then as now, potato crisps were a popular snack. There were only two big suppliers, Smith's and Blue Bird. Each had large delivery vans, always in immaculate condition and with beautiful and intricate logos emblazoned on the sides. Also, there were several novelty vehicles, such as that advertising Worthington beer. It was in the shape of a bottle of beer, and can be seen today in the Bass Museum in Burton-on-Trent.

There were usually long queues in the General Post Office in Howard Street, and no wonder. The long counter was split into many specialist service areas, so at one you could purchase stamps, at another telegrams, another postal orders and so on. Therefore, it was heaven help you if you wished to send a telegram, buy a stamp and a postal order, for you had to queue three times. It was certainly a frustrating and time-consuming system, designed purely for the benefit of the counter staff. It should be said, though, that the telegraph service was excellent. Very few people had a telephone, so the telegraph service was in great demand. As soon as a telegram was received at the post office, it was sealed in an envelope and quickly delivered by one of the telegraph boys on his bicycle. They wore a blue uniform made of thick material, and their cycles were very substantial affairs, painted red. During the war, of course, the arrival of a telegram was an unwelcome event, for it often announced the death of a loved one. However, before the war it was exciting to be a recipient. The service faded in the post war years, as private and public telephones became more common. The first public telephone box that I saw was situated at the corner of Demesne Road and Westmoreland Road. It had the same shape as the familiar red boxes, but it was made of sand-coloured cement, with red glazing bars. I think it looked better than the later all-red ones. It was erected in about 1935. The parcel post also flourished before the war. The Post Office had numerous large, red painted vans to cope with the huge demand. The rates were very cheap, so people could afford to use the service prodigally, unlike today. At Christmas, the service was near to collapse with the sheer volume of business. I recall laughing at a cartoon which featured a parcel sorting office. It showed harassed employees sorting the parcels into skips, and on one parcel was written, 'FRAGILE. PLEASE THROW UNDER-ARM.'

Wool-made garments have a distressing tendency to develop holes, particularly the heels of socks and stockings. Consequently, a never-ending task for a housewife was darning, i.e., repairing the holes. As children we not only wore darned stockings, but also patched trousers. Clothes had to last as long as possible, which was why, when buying a new Sunday-best serge suit, my mother always bought one that was much too large, so that I could 'grow into it'. Another time-consuming activity for the ladies was knitting. Every single female that I knew had been able to knit since childhood. The art probably reached its peak during the war, when everyone seemed to be knitting for the forces. Sadly, like so much else, it is now largely a lost art.

In most homes, a treasured possession was a button box. Usually this was a tin box containing a large and varied assortment of beautiful and intricate buttons. If I had nothing else to do, I would empty the tin onto the table and sort the contents of our collection, particularly the military ones. Another item kept by most families was the photo box. Rarely were photographs kept in albums; rather, a shoebox would do. So a popular pastime was to empty the sepia photographs on to the table and sort and identify the people on them.

Wallpapering was a messy and delicate task. My parents could only afford very cheap paper, so it had to be handled with care. It had a border along the length of each side, so at least one border had to be trimmed. To do this, Dad sat on a chair with his feet outstretched, nursing the roll in the crook of his feet. Then one edge of the paper was trimmed as straight as he could manage. The paste used was made of flour and water, so care was needed to keep smears off the front of the paper, as every smear was obvious. The paper stretched and tore easily as it was being hung, so you will understand that the few times that I remember my father being bad tempered was when he was wall papering.

Whist drives were popular with the older people. My parents went to one or two each week. I was always surprised, when they came home after attending one, how earnestly my mother would say that so and so should have trumped someone else's king, and so on. I could not believe that anyone took the game so seriously. As a rule, younger people did not go near whist drives - they were more into dancing. In addition, the various church halls were more used then than now. There were concerts and magic lantern shows in them as well as dances. In fact, the church was much more a part of the social life of the town than is now the case.

On the corner of Drumgold Street and Duke Street there was a large and high-class shop called T H Cowin's for the sale of ladies wear. On the corner of the shop, facing Strand Street, it had a magnificent large, curved window. Unfortunately, it was in a vulnerable spot, so from time to time it ended up in pieces, although the damage was always accidental. On the opposite corner stood a large gents outfitter's called the Fifty-Shilling Tailor. Here you could buy a three-piece suit, made-to-measure, for just two pounds and ten shillings, i.e., fifty shillings. Another comparable shop was Alexandre's, whilst the stylish Burton's was in Victoria Street. Its window displays were very elegant. The dummies were all immaculately dressed, some in lounge suits, some in casual wear and some in dinner jackets. There was also a selection of suitable accessories on display, such as silk scarves, top hats, canes and so on. I used to gaze at the excellent display and wonder whether I would ever be able to afford to wear such fine clothes. There were various other good shops catering for the needs of ladies and gents, so the Douglas residents were well served.

As it is now nearly fifty years since I lived on the Island, I am in the fortunate position of time standing still regarding my memory of the place. I have not become confused by the gradual alterations that have taken place since then. I recall clearly places such as Makin's chip shop, the Palais de Danse, The Picture House, Strand Cinema, Sisson and Johnson's toy shops, Feldman's, Gore's rock shop, Maley's the chemist and so on. They are now all gone, and with it a little elegance and charm has been lost.

CHAPTER EIGHT

WARTIME

And The Angels Sing

The day war broke out was a beautiful, sunny, Sunday morning. Today people might say, 'What were you doing when John F Kennedy was assassinated?' Well, to my generation it would be more appropriate to ask what we were doing when war was declared. I was standing in the front room of twenty-eight, listening to the wireless. I suppose that almost everyone in the land was listening to that fateful broadcast. It was 11.15 on September 3rd 1939. The Prime Minister was speaking and I still recall some of his words, ' I am speaking to you from the Cabinet Room at 10 Downing Street. This morning, the British ambassador in Berlin handed the German government a final note stating that unless we heard from them at 11 o'clock that they were prepared at once to withdraw their troops from Poland, a state of war would exist between us. I have to tell you now that no such undertaking has been received, and that consequently this country is at war with Germany...' The speech went on for a few minutes more.

My mother burst into tears, and said, "What will happen to George?" He was not present, but, at nineteen, he would be the first of us to be called up for service. Dad was silent for a while, and then put his arms around mother's shoulders in a rare show of tenderness. He said quietly "Come on, Bertha, don't get upset. Everything will be alright." Bertha was his pet name for my mother. I recall saying something stupid about wishing that I were old enough to join the forces straight away.

The transition from peace to war was not as dramatic as one might suppose. Conscription of young men started, identity cards were issued and we were obliged to carry our gas masks in their little brown cardboard boxes. All that sort of thing quickly became established as normal, but much of our daily lives remained untouched. Food was plentiful, and life went on pretty much as before except, of course, the visitors quickly disappeared and the Manx Grand Prix races were cancelled. The passenger liner Athenia, with 1400 people on board, was torpedoed and sunk in the Atlantic on the first day, and HMS Courageous, an aircraft carrier, was sunk within a few days of the war declaration. The terrible loss of HMS Royal Oak happened in October, so, although our daily lives were not much affected, the ugliness of war was soon apparent to all.

My brother, George, volunteered for the Royal Navy straight away, and served on minesweepers and corvettes. He became an ASDIC operator. At the time I had no idea what ASDIC was, but it has featured in so many films such as The Cruel Sea, that now everyone knows about it. My next eldest brother, Charles, was living in Leyland, and worked on bomber production at Dick Kerr's in Preston. He became a foreman, and worked there throughout the war. Many of the Halifax bombers were made there. My eldest brother, Ernie, was medically unfit for service, so he promptly joined the newly formed Local Defence Volunteers, usually known as the LDV. Quickly this was translated to Look, Duck and Vanish. The name was then changed to the Home Guard, but is now better known as Dad's

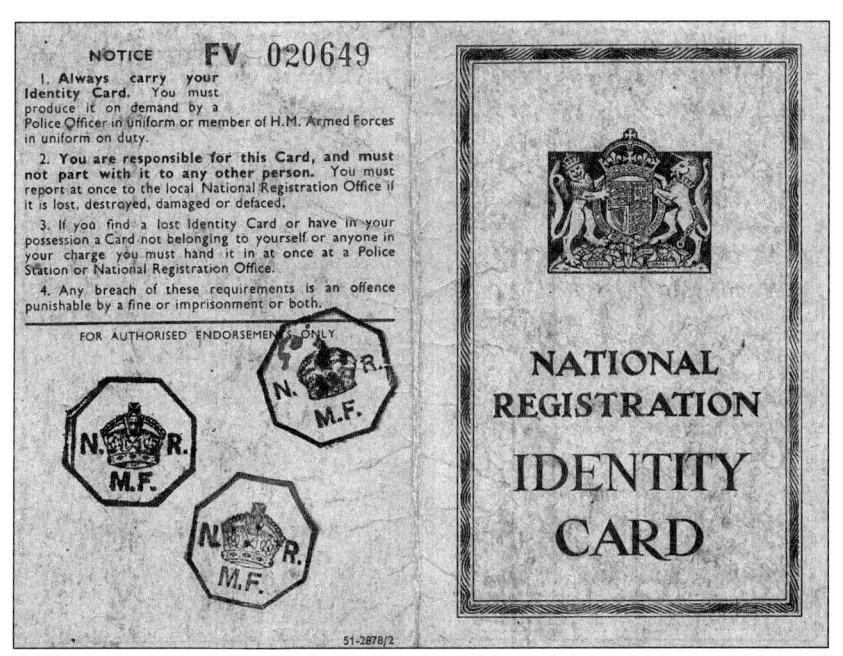

Every civilian in the land was issued with an Identity Card at the outbreak of World War Two. They remained in use until about 1955.

My brothers George and Ernie, with Emmy, (Ernie's wife), and my mother, taken about 1942. Ernie is in his Home Guard uniform.

Army. Sadly, Ernie died of a heart complaint in 1945. Meanwhile my remaining brother, Harry, joined the army so, when later I joined the RAF, my family had members in the army, the navy, the air force and a reserved occupation.

Novelty dances were all the rage before and during the war. One of the first popular wartime songs was We're Going to Hang Out the Washing on the Siegfried Line, and the dance involved doing a lot of goose-stepping and giving Nazi salutes - we thought it was hilarious, and joined in with great enthusiasm. The dance halls were always crowded and, of course, there was a huge influx of new faces, particularly servicemen and women. The Harold Moorhouse band was resident at the Palais de Danse, but at the Villa Marina, it became common to have other bands as well as the established Steve Lahmas trio. They were usually service bands, and some of them were very good. The usual admission charge was three shillings (18p), and the dances were from seven-thirty until twelve o'clock. The local star performer on the dance floor was 'Count' Cringle. He was an excellent dancer, but soon had serious rivals in the form of various army, navy and air force personnel. It was heaven for the young girls to suddenly have all of these new and exciting people around. Generally, the Palais was frequented by officers and officer cadets. The Villa was more favoured by the other ranks. My crowd went to the Villa. These were the two main ballrooms, but there was also the delightful Collinson's Café ballroom for private functions. It, like that at the Palais, had a sprung floor, which made it ideal for dancing. There were also regular and cheap dances in the church halls, such as those at St. Matthews and the Catholic Hall in Myrtle Street. Later, in about 1942, the Derby Castle ballroom was opened for dancing on Sunday afternoons. Only service members in uniform were admitted, so we donned our ATC uniforms to get in. Admission was free, which we thought was a jolly good idea.

Up to the outbreak of war the music played on the BBC was all by British bands, such as those led by Geraldo, Harry Roy,

Ambrose and lots of others. Recordings of American bands and singers such as Bing Crosby were also heard, but soon the American influence became much stronger. Meanwhile the ranks of the British bands were thinned as their members were called up. However, on the plus side, this meant that excellent service bands were formed. The best and most famous of these was the superb RAF Squadronaires dance band, formed almost entirely of ex-Ambrose bandmen.

Another change was that radio comedy shows became much more common. There were only two wireless channels, the Home and Forces programmes. Comedy programmes such as ITMA (It's That Man Again) became popular Sunday entertainment, which had hitherto been very dull days. Request programmes were naturally in great demand, as were the American shows with comedians like Bob Hope. Singing groups like the Andrews Sisters were heard for the first time, and bands such as those of Glenn Miller and Arty Shaw. Vera Lynn and Ann Shelton were the most popular British singers.

Many of the wireless broadcasts were from 'somewhere in England' and weather forecasts were suspended for the duration. The newsreaders always started their bulletins by announcing their name. So, one might hear, 'This is the six o'clock news, and this is Alvar Lidell reading it.' From Germany, the broadcasts of Lord Haw Haw started. He was British, but born in the US. His name was William Joyce. He broadcast propaganda for the enemy throughout the war, but no attempt was made to jam his programmes, largely because he was regarded as something of a comedian, although he also spread some fear. He was captured at the end of the war, and hanged.

The BBC broadcasts to the occupied countries made unintelligible but compulsive listening. The programmes started with drumbeats that went 'bom, bom, bom, boom'. In Morse code, this was dot, dot, dot, dash, the symbol for V for an Allied victory. This was followed by the rousing music of Lillebolero, and then the messages personnels. These were messages being passed to resistance fighters. Each message was read slowly and then repeated even more slowly to allow the message to be written down. A typical message might be, 'The rose will bloom again. The - rose - will - bloom - again.' The messages would be read for about a half an hour, and I often wondered what drama lay behind these enigmatic lines.

At the cinemas, the British films always showed the final credits against a background of a Union Flag flying proudly in the breeze. In the foyer, suitably patriotic messages were displayed. At the Picture House, they had the framed Shakespearean quotation:
'Come three corners of the World in arms,
And we shall shock them; naught shall make us rue,
If England to herself be true.'

Another one was:
This England never did, nor never shall,
Lie at the proud foot of a conqueror.

Also displayed was a silhouette of a Lancaster bomber, with the message, 'There is room for you in this aircraft'. This was followed by the afterthought in small print, 'The maximum age for aircrew is thirty-two.'

Before the war several diseases were prevalent that are now hardly given a thought. For example, diphtheria, tuberculosis (TB), mumps, measles, whooping cough, scarlet fever and others. In Britain penicillin was developed and shared with America, but not Germany. It proved to be a spectacular advance in medicine, and was used for the effective treatment of a whole raft of diseases, including VD. On the other hand, almost everyone smoked. Cigarettes were the most common, but smoking of pipes and cigars was also widespread, along with, to a lesser extent, snuff-taking. Ladies often smoked cigarettes, one of the most popular brands for them being De Reske Minors. For men the top brands were Player's Navy Cut, Wills' Star, Kensitas, Woodbines, Player's Weights and many others. At the cinema it was always interesting to look up and watch the light from the projector fighting its way to the screen through the dense fog of cigarette smoke. Lung cancer may have been common, but the connection with smoking had not been made, so we all puffed away merrily.

440 Squadron of the Air Training Corps, the ATC, was formed in 1940. The Squadron Commander was Cecil Watterson, and other officers included Mr. Skillicorn, Peter Hyslop and Warrant Officer 'Tishy' Kelly. A notice had appeared in the Times and the Examiner, stating that any young people who were interested in the RAF should go along to a meeting at the Town Hall to hear the details. I went along and, in common with about thirty other boys, put my name down to join the Douglas 'Town' squadron. Another squadron was formed at the Douglas High School, and great, but friendly, rivalry existed between us. Similarly, there was the Army Cadet Force for those interested in joining the army. Between them, of course, they spelled the death of organisations such as the Boy Scouts, until the end of the war. Everyone that I knew was in one of the cadet units. Being in the ATC involved us attending about four evening parades each week, plus Sunday parades. Sometimes the one on Sunday merely involved marching along the promenade as an adjunct to a service parade. This was o.k. but not really very exciting. The excitement came when we visited Fort Island and fired Lewis and Vickers machine guns, Thompson (Tommy) guns and rifles.

Even better, was to visit Andreas where an Australian Spitfire squadron was stationed. I recall one visit in particular. It was a beautiful Sunday afternoon, and we were at one of the dispersal points. Here we were able to sit in the Spitfires, which were fuelled and armed - all ready to go, in fact. I was sitting in the cockpit of one of the machines, my imagination in overdrive, when a flight lieutenant casually said,' By the way, try not to push this little chap', the 'little chap' being the gun firing button. Although it was set to 'safe', I marvelled how casual he was about it. Later, the Flight Commander called us together, and told us that they had shot down a

I joined the Air Training Corps as soon as it was formed, and became a flight sergeant in the 'town' squadron. My predecessor was Jeff Forester, who became a pilot and a squadron leader.

German aircraft that morning. In addition, he had obtained permission for the flight to put on a special display for our benefit. However, he had been warned not to fly too low. The pilots walked nonchalantly to their Spitfires, and soon were airborne in grand style. They climbed into the wild blue yonder and disappeared from view. The stillness and silence became quite eerie, and we wondered where they could have gone. Suddenly we almost died of fright, for the aircraft roared over the hedge near us in line astern and at full throttle. They were so low that they had to climb to clear the hedge. They roared over our heads toward the airfield, turned and headed back to us again, still at nought feet. They were brilliant. This private air show went on for some time, and I shall remember it until I die.

However, even better than our visits to Andreas were those to Jurby, where we could actually fly. The very first aircraft in which I flew was a Blenheim bomber, and the experience was unforgettable. Everything was so strange and exciting that first time - the terrific engine noise, the cramped crew space, the cold draughts and, above all, the sheer delight of flying. Whilst in the ATC I went on to fly in various other aircraft, including the Hereford, Hampden, Lysander, Beaufort and others.

I must have done all right as a cadet, because after a short while I was promoted to corporal, followed soon after by promotion to sergeant and finally to flight sergeant, the highest rank attainable to a cadet. The previous flight sergeant was Jeff Forester, who left to join the RAF in 1941. His brother, Peter, was also in the ATC, and they both went on to become pilots. Peter flew in Lancaster's. The Forrester family owned the Port Soderick entertainments, as well as the pleasure boat Karina.

It was whilst I was in the ATC that I met several boys who became very good friends; people such as Arnold Breadner, who became a Spitfire pilot and was Best Man at my wedding, Les Hewitt, Harold Jergasson and many others. We also got to know the members of the

High School squadron, such as 'Spike' Hughes, Lennie Watterson, 'Bing' Crosby, Fred Kennish and various others. Then there were others, such as 'Cap' Cain in the Army Cadets, Stan Quine, Peter Daugherty and Tommy Williams. Tommy and another friend, Billy Cain, were destined to die in the Winter Hill aeroplane crash in the 1950's. Fred Kennish was injured, but recovered and went on to become the Mayor of Douglas in 1990.

Each Saturday a group of us went to the dance at the Villa Marina. I suppose there would be a total of about ten boys and ten girls, such as Adeline Quayle, Jean Cowin and Renee Corrin. I used to 'go out' with Adeline, but it was common to have floating relationships within the group. Thus, the girlfriend of one boy would start 'going out' with someone else. No one fell out over this arrangement. So, Adeline and I drifted apart, and I started to go out with Elsie Ash (who later married Billy Cain) and then it was back to Adeline.

Dances were held every evening except Sundays, and one time in 1941 I went to the Villa with my cousin John Gill. As was the usual custom, we patrolled the walkway behind the balcony seats looking for likely partners. Two girls of about our age were sitting on the back row, one blonde and the other with dark hair. John, who was taller than me, said he would ask the blonde and I the other one. The 'other one' was a good-looking girl who was a little shorter than I was. She wore a black, short-sleeved dress, which had a white collar and cuffs with red spots. She was a charming girl and we got on very well. We became friends, but I lost contact with her when she joined the WAAF in 1942. I certainly did not realise it then, but she was destined to become my wife in 1949. Meanwhile, as I said, we lost contact with one another apart from a few letters, and they soon petered out.

On Sunday evenings, most of us, boys and girls, went to the Picture House. There were enough of us to fill the whole of the back

I met my future wife in 1941, but we lost contact when she joined the WAAF. This picture was taken in 1943. We married in 1949.

row of the seats in the balcony. Often we did not even know what film was to be shown. About fifteen minutes before the start of the film the words of popular songs were displayed on the screen, and the whole audience sang along to the organ music, and always the last song was Ellan Vannin. It was at this time that I was given a white feather. I was walking along Allan Street one evening on my own. Walking along in the other direction was a woman aged about thirty. As we passed she handed me a white feather without saying a word, and went piously on her way. She had probably been reading The Four Feathers or a similar novel. Anyway, I was not in the least put out. In fact, I laughed to myself as I thought how anxious I was to get into the RAF.

My particular friend at that time was Les Hewitt, and as soon as I was seventeen (1942), we enlisted for flying duties together. Les was slightly older than I, but had waited until I was old enough so that we could join and, hopefully, train together. We signed on at Noble's Hall. That was the last time that we did anything together in the RAF. He was always a little ahead of me. Shortly after enlisting, I was sent to Renshaw Hall in Liverpool for my medical examination and initial selection interviews. From there, it was off to RAF Burtonwood for aircrew aptitude tests and more examinations. Toward the end of the process all of us who had lasted that far, were ushered into a large room. There was a substantial crowd of us, but we had only been there a couple of minutes when an airman called my name. My heart sank, as I felt certain that I would be told that I had been rejected. In fact, it turned out that he came from Pulrose, and he was pleased to see another Manxie. He explained that he was the clerk to the Squadron Leader who was to give us our final interview, and he would ensure that I was called early. In addition, he would be sure to pass on the intelligence that I was very suitable-looking aircrew material. Well, I do not know about the second bit, but sure enough, I was the first person called for interview. The interview with the squadron leader went well, and he said that from my various assessments I seemed a suitable person for PNB (Pilot,

Navigator, Bomb-aimer) training. I was to return home and await my formal call-up to the RAF.

I returned to Fleetwood and sailed for home on the Ben my Chree, but we had not gone a hundred yards before we ran aground. It was only on mud, so presented no problems, except that we would have to wait for the tide to go out and then back again before proceeding. It was therefore the early hours of the morning before we docked in Douglas.

Most of the crowd that I knocked about with was waiting to go into the forces. A group of us decided that it would be a good idea if, during the summer of 1942, we had a holiday together. However, where could we go? Clearly, it had to be a do-it-yourself sort of thing, as we had no money and in any case, there were very few places available. Suddenly someone had a brainwave. Stan Quayle had been a big wheel in the local Boy Scout movement before the war, so he would be able to borrow a tent and all the other paraphernalia that would be required for camping. Another member of the group called Stan Quine knew a farmer at Knocksharry, about two miles north of Peel, who would let us camp on his land free of charge, so things began to take shape very nicely. The next problem was food. Two of the group worked in a grocery shop, so they were able to set aside various things such as tins of soup, some sugar, porridge and so on, so although we would not have any feasts, at least we could eat well, considering wartime rationing and shortages. There remained one last hurdle. How could we get the gear and ourselves to Knocksharry? Petrol was rationed and, in any case, none of us could drive a lorry. However, all was not lost. Although he did not knock about with us, we all knew Jack Corlett well. Jack, like the rest of us, was waiting to go into the RAF. In fact, he became a flight lieutenant air gunner. His father had a haulage business, and had a contract to do work at Jurby, so we asked him whether he could borrow one of the lorries one Sunday and drive us to Peel. 'No problem.' he assured us, so all was set for a last, wonderful, carefree holiday, as soon we would all be going our separate ways into an uncertain future. Although never mentioned, I am sure that at some time each of us looked at the others and wondered how many of us would be alive by the end of the war. It is hard to appreciate now, just how huge was the question mark that hung over the future of each of us. However, none of this mattered on that beautiful, sunny, Sunday morning in August, as we loaded our provisions and ourselves onto the lorry.

Our current girlfriends joined us, sitting astride the tent and other gear. I recall Mildred McKibbon, Jean Cowin, Dorothy Quaggin, Joan Lee and Renee Corrin. They were coming along for the ride, and to see that we had at least one good meal, which they would cook, before returning to Douglas with Jack that evening. They would come out to us again on Thursday afternoon, which was half-closing day, and Jack would come back on Sunday to help to clear the site and get us home. The campers were Stan (Velvet lips) Quine, Les Hewitt, Stan Quayle, Dennis (Cap) Cain, Tommy Williams, Cliff Young, Brian Taggart and me. I was the last person to be picked up. I had a leather suitcase packed with clothes, and I threw it on to the back of the lorry. The suitcase, like many of the clothes, belonged to George Broad, but as he had been called up to the RAF the previous year, I reasoned that he would not mind. I climbed aboard and, before we set off, someone took a photograph of us all. It is strange now, to think how casual and unimportant it seemed at the time, but that photograph is now one of my most prized possessions. Almost all of the people on it have long since gone out of my life and, sadly, some of them are dead.

Under Stan Quayle's guidance we somehow managed to erect the tent, whilst the girls did a fine job of cooking a good meal, so everything augured well for the coming week. So it turned out. Various things went wrong, of course, but that is what we expected. For example, the following day we found that the hens had pecked at the bag of oatmeal and scattered it all over the floor of the tent. We scooped it up as best we could, and resolved to organise the food

'All aboard for Knocksharry!' This was the start of an unforgettable holiday in 1942. The girls included Mildred McKibbon, Jean Cowin, Dorothy Quaggin, Joan Lee and Renee Corrin.

'The campers.' L to R: Stan Quayle; Cliff Young; Tommy Williams; Dennis 'Cap' Cain; Stan 'Velvet lips' Quine; Les Hewitt; Allan Gill.

store in a better manner. It was decided to put all the tinned food in one of the cases. It had to be a strong one, of course, so mine (or, rather, George Broad's) was chosen. However, it proved unequal to the task, for when someone tried to lift it the bottom fell out. On another occasion, Tommy Williams was making the meal (six tins of soup), and he decided that it could do with a little pepper. Unfortunately, the top came off the canister, so the whole lot went in. The soup smelled delicious, but tasted like fire. Rather than waste the soup he decided to dilute it with another six, with the result that we now had twelve tins of undrinkable soup. Reluctantly, we had to throw it all under the hedge. It was a wonderful holiday, filled with laughs and never a cross word the whole time. It exceeded all of our expectations.

On the Saturday it was important that we all went to Douglas, for two reasons: to collect our pay (10/- or 50p in my case) and to go to the Villa that evening. It poured with rain, so we set off in twos to have a better chance of getting a lift. I went with 'Cap' Cain, and we had walked to Peel and about a mile towards Douglas before we were offered a lift in a van loaded with boxes of kippers. We were soaked to the skin by this time, so were grateful for the ride. By the time that we got to Douglas we smelled strongly of kippers, so when I went into Lawton's for my pay everyone went 'Phewwww'. It was the same when I got home. In fact it was worse, because my brother Charles and his wife had come to stay with us for a holiday, and had arrived just before I got home. They were a charming, tidy and orderly couple, so must have been quite revolted by my smelly and scruffy appearance. However, after a hot bath I felt and smelled a lot better. Even so, that evening at the Villa the girls had a grand time asking me if I had kippers for tea. After the dance we returned to Peel on the train and walked the remainder of the way. The next day we broke camp and, as he had promised, Jack came in the lorry to take us home. It had really been a super time. It had been a happy, relaxed and memorable week, one which, I fecl sure, none of us ever forgot.

Shortly after the camp our numbers began to dwindle as one and then another was called-up. 'Cap' Cain joined the Argyle and Sutherland Highlanders, Cliff Young the Fleet Air Arm, Stan Quine the army, and so on. Early in 1943, my friend Harold Jergasson was called to the RAF and began training as an air gunner. On his last Saturday before leaving the Island, we were as usual at a dance at the Villa. He suggested that we two should go to the Central Hotel for a bon voyage drink, which I was pleased to do. Harold ordered two bottles of Castletown Blue Label beer (5d a bottle), but the Irish barmaid refused to serve him, as she said he was too young. She would, however, serve me, although, in fact, I was even younger than Harold. Anyway, we got our drinks and had a good laugh about it. A couple of days later he left the Island to join the RAF. His training lasted six weeks, after which he became a sergeant and joined an operational squadron. He was killed on his first operation. I told the barmaid about his death and she cried.

Meanwhile, my father had been selected to serve on the Military Service Tribunal in the early days of the war. Its function was to assess the applicant's case for exemption or deferment from service with the armed forces. Many people, of course, had perfectly valid reasons for wishing to be exempted. It was a very important tribunal, and was chaired by the High Bailiff, Mr. Ramsey Johnson. He and my father became good friends. Dad was proud of his position, and he worked conscientiously to do a good job. He rarely talked about any of the cases he dealt with, and even if he did, it was only in the most general terms. One day, though, he said that he had told someone who he felt was just trying to dodge military service, 'I have one son in the navy, one in the army and another (me) breaking his neck to get into the RAF! Dad remained on the tribunal until the end of the war.

The pilots from Andreas and Jurby put on some entertaining displays, both official and unofficial, from time to time. At the conclusion of the Remembrance service at the War Memorial in 1942,

The Military Service Tribunal. The Chairman is High Bailiff Ramsey Johnson. My father is on the extreme right of the picture. (Courtesy of Manx National Heritage)

three Spitfires in 'vic' formation flew towards us from offshore at low level. They had to climb to clear the War Memorial as they performed their impressive salute to the fallen. Another memory is of standing at the promenade railings near the sunken gardens. The shore was about twenty feet below and, from time to time, a Blenheim or Anson would be flown below the level of the promenade and along the curve of the sea wall, so you could look down at the aircraft as it roared past. I admired the young aircrews immensely.

When I worked at the internment camp, we were not allowed in until the roll call was completed, so it was usually just a little before nine o'clock before we could enter. Nine o'clock was also the departure time for the daily sailing to Liverpool or Fleetwood by the passenger ship. The vessel would leave the harbour, sailing astern, before turning in the bay and setting off. At this time it was a common sight to see a Jurby aircraft 'shoot-up' the ship whilst this was going on. It must have been quite exciting for the aircrew. However, one morning it was very misty, so I could not see the ship from the camp. Suddenly there was a muffled explosion, and my immediate thought was that the ship had gone aground on the rocks. Later, when the mist had cleared, there was no sign of the ship, so I put the matter out of my head. It was many years later, when I spoke to my future wife about the incident, that I learned what had happened. She was in the WAAF, and was returning from leave that day, so she was aboard the vessel. As was so common, the aircraft 'attacked' them in the bay, but this time with disastrous results. The aircraft struck the water (that was the boom that I had heard) and began to sink. A boat was quickly lowered, and the crew removed from the stricken aeroplane. Every member of the crew was dead, except for one young aviator. He was brought on board the ship in a dazed and barely conscious condition. This heart-rending incident did not even warrant a tiny footnote in the annals of the war.

Later, my wife was stationed at Jurby, and she told me of another sad story from that time. An Avro Anson was on a training flight, and crashed into Snaefell. All the crew members, except one, were killed. Both of the survivor's legs were broken and, presumably shocked and disorientated, he was obliged to crawl all the way to Laxey to raise the alarm and obtain assistance. You would think that he would have been rescued quickly, as it seems inconceivable that anyone could go missing on such a small mountain. However, the weather was foul, and it was dark, so the journey must have been a nightmare for him. The loss of life in Training Command was quite high.

During the blitz on Liverpool, a notice appeared in the Manx papers. It was an appeal for people to 'adopt' children who had been made orphans by the raids. My brother Ernie and his wife, Emmy, were childless, and promptly offered to take one of them. That was how Joan came to live with them. She was about a year old, and Ernie and Emmy loved her. However, as she was declared an orphan, they could not formally adopt her, but she grew up in a secure and happy home. Years later the bombshell came, when Joan was sixteen. Her parents appeared from nowhere, and demanded that Joan return to live with them in Liverpool. Emmy, who was a widow by this time, was devastated, and Joan was furious; but she was legally obliged to go. As soon as she was eighteen, though, she left Liverpool and returned to live with Emmy. Joan still lives in the Isle of Man.

CHAPTER NINE

LIFE IN THE RAF

*If I only had wings,
A tiny pair of those elusive things.*

Wartime song.

In 1943, Les Hewitt was called up, and shortly afterwards I, too, was ordered to report to the RAF at Lords Cricket Ground. This was the Aircrew Reception Centre, (A.C.R.C.), known throughout the service as Arsy-Tarsy. It was the first time in my life that I had visited London, and I was horrified at the bomb damage that was apparent everywhere. There were hundreds of cadets at Lords, but soon we had been checked-in and allocated billets. I was assigned to stay in a block of luxury flats called Abbey Lodge in St. John's Wood. The rooms were large and comfortable, the bathrooms had marble floors and the taps were gold plated. I thought, 'Not bad for my first billet.' There were five of us in one room, including three Allan's -

Allan Love, Dave Allan and I. For convenience we were each given a nickname. Mine was Cobby, the name of a character in a cowboy film showing at the time. Soon, though, Cobby was corrupted to Cobber, and the name stuck. Arsy-Tarsy was where documentation and medical examinations were carried out; one of which was a hearing test. From my previous tests I knew that my left ear was suspect - possibly I had a punctured eardrum. It was only by luck that I got through the earlier test, so I was anxious about the prospect of another. About twenty of us were lined up at one end of a room, and the Medical Officer was at the other. He whispered words to the cadet at the front of the queue. The cadet stood sideways with, say, his left ear towards the officer. Meanwhile, another cadet had been detailed to put his finger in the other ear. When it came to my turn, I looked pleadingly at him, and he obligingly kept his finger well clear, so I was just able to make out what was being whispered. To this day, I am grateful to that unknown cadet for his kindness. It was the last ear test that I had in the service. In fact, when later I was a flight sergeant, my skipper wanted to put me forward for a commission, but I declined, as there was a possibility that I would be required to have another ear test. To jump ahead, after I had been demobilised I tried to rejoin the service, but was failed, because of a punctured eardrum, something that I had suspected.

Meanwhile, back at ACRC, we were issued with our kit, and started basic training. This involved a lot of marching, and once I even saw Les marching, but in the opposite direction. Meals were served in a mess located in a nearby park. However, you could not just go to the mess; you had to go on a meal parade and march there. The breakfast parade was at seven o'clock, so the five of us quickly decided that it was preferable to have a lie in bed and miss breakfast. Thus, one morning we were all lying cosily in our beds when Corporal Macklethwaite entered the room. He seemed quite friendly as he asked if we were comfortable, to which we assured him that the answer was yes. Then, without warning, he tipped each of us out of bed and on to the floor, in quick succession.

"Why aren't you on parade?"
"Because we don't want any breakfast, corporal"
"In that case you will attend the parade, wait until the others have finished, and then you will march back with them."
"But what is the point?"
"The point is that you are now in the RAF and that is what you will do."

The first church parade was held the following Sunday morning. We all stood in line whilst the corporal shouted, 'Fall-in here, the C of E's.' Promptly a number of chaps did as he ordered. Then, in a similar manner, he separated the Catholics and the Jews. To the few who remained, he said, "Fall-in here, the O D's." That left just a couple of cadets.
"What are you two - atheists?"
"No, corporal, we are Methodists."
"Well, you silly little airmen, Methodists ARE OD's - Other Denominations, get it?"
"Yes, corporal."
Next came our first kit inspection. We had our kit carefully laid out on our beds and felt quite proud to have mastered at least this little bit of RAF life. The corporal inspected the kit of all five of us, and we waited to be praised for our efforts:
"Where are your razors? Not one of you has one in his kit."
"We don't shave, corporal."
"I didn't ask whether you shaved. I said where are your razors?"
"We weren't issued with one, corporal."
"You're expected to buy your own. See to it by tomorrow."

There seemed to be so much to learn that we despaired of ever mastering the requirements of the service. Soon I was to learn another. I developed quite bad toothache, so one lunchtime, instead of going to the mess, I strolled into the dental surgery. The dentist was a flight lieutenant, and he asked me what I wanted. I told him I had toothache, and would he mind looking at my teeth. He asked me why

I had not reported sick that morning so I said that I was not sick, I just had toothache. The dentist laughed and explained the correct sick parade procedure. However, as I was there anyway, he looked at my teeth. He said that one of them would have to come out. After the extraction my mouth felt much better. As I left the surgery, he said, 'Next time, report sick.'

A few days later we were marched to Seymour Hall. The place was crowded, so there must have been a couple of thousand cadets there. We sat at tables and each of us was handed a long list of examination questions. They were all simple, such as 'Put the following six names in alphabetical order', but there were so many questions that it was impossible to do them all in the allotted time. The idea was to do as many as you could. Now we had no idea what this was for, and nobody chose to tell us. When we were called-up, it was for pre-aircrew training (PACT), which consisted of going to school for six months. It turned out that the Seymour Hall examination had been to find suitable cadets to miss the PACT course and go straight to Initial Training Wing (ITW). In those days, we lived in a world of initials. Anyway, I must have performed well in the examination, as I was one of about twenty cadets selected to go forward for interview, from which six lucky ones would be picked. The interviewing officer was a flight lieutenant. I entered the room with some trepidation, as by this time I realised that it was something special. However, I need not have worried. As soon as I sat down he said, 'I see that you come from the Isle of Man.' From there on he reminisced about a particularly rewarding holiday he had there in 1939, only stopping from time to time to ask me the odd question about the Island. I must have impressed him, because I was one of the six selected to proceed straight to ITW out of the large crowd that sat the examination. Certainly, my Manx connections were paying-off handsomely for me in the RAF.

Therefore, I reported to 10 ITW at Scarborough. My billet was in a private hotel, called the Saint Nicholas. True, it was a step down from Abbey Lodge, but still very comfortable. I marvelled that the RAF actually paid me to lead such an exciting life in such comfortable surroundings. My particular friend there was Del Finnet. Del was one of life's natural winners - he had everything going for him. He was about five foot-ten, was a good-looking chap, and had worked in the Air Ministry. He talked quite casually about very high-ranking officers with whom he had come into contact. He was a loyal friend and good company. We always went about together. Upon arrival at ITW, Del had been selected to be the Cadet Leader - he was that sort of chap. Everything that we did in the way of training seemed to come easily to him, whereas Archie Simpson, our other friend, and I had to struggle to keep up. One of the problems with being with someone like Del, though, was that when we went to a dance, I always ended up with 'her friend'. He trained as a navigator in Canada and, of course, was commissioned. We only met once after leaving Scarborough, and that was in 1947. We spent an entertaining evening recounting our adventures since our days at ITW. I do not know what became of him after that, but I expect he was very successful in his chosen career.

Our two main instructors were pompous flight lieutenants who were ex- schoolteachers. They had no sense of humour and treated us like pupils. We called them Tweedle Dee and Tweedle Dum. On the other hand, our drill sergeant, a chap called Adams, was friendly, and he had a real regard for us. In fact, he intended to re-muster to aircrew himself. Most of the subjects that we studied were of interest, such as navigation, Morse code, aircraft recognition, care of weapons and so on. A few, such as gas precautions and foot drill were boring. Twice a week we were marched to the local castle for weapons training, and that was great fun. Sometimes we would do clay pigeon shooting, using shotguns. At other times, it would be rifle shooting or using Sten guns. The Sten gun was most unpredictable, and had an alarming habit of either stopping whilst you were firing it, or starting when you were not. I recall the time when several of us were facing the targets, each armed with a Sten gun. The corporal said, "If your gun stops, keep pointing it at the target and raise your hand. I will come and sort the problem out." Sure enough, we were all merrily firing away at the targets, not hitting much, as usual, when one of the Sten's had a stoppage. However, the cadet did not raise his hand. Instead he turned to the corporal, and as he did so, all of us came in line with the gun. Courage instantly disappeared, as we all, including the corporal, fell flat on our faces in the mud, leaving just one person standing. A thing that always amazed me was, whenever we used weapons, we just drew them from the armoury all oiled and cleaned. After firing the guns, we just handed them back, often covered in mud, for the armourers to clean. They must have hated us cadets.

My weight had been eight and a half stone when I joined the service, but by now it had gone up to ten and a half stone, thanks to good living, enough exercise and plenty of sleep. One thing that I detested, though, was the necessity to swim a hundred yards. It seems that after ditching in the sea, some aircrew had been lost because they could not swim to the dinghy. Hence, the edict went out that all aircrew must demonstrate that they could swim this minimum distance. If you could do it you were graded an 'X' swimmer. If you could manage anything between zero and a hundred yards you were a 'Y' swimmer and those who could not swim at all were 'Z' swimmers, so twice a week the dreaded order was given, 'Fall-in the Y and Z swimmers.' We were marched to the Scarborough swimming baths where, floundering about with just our identity discs on, we tried to swim the required distance. Meanwhile, the non-swimmers fared even worse. They had to wear a Mae West life jacket and jump in from the diving board. They then had to struggle to the poolside as best they could. The Mae West was then handed to another cadet for him to repeat the performance. The trouble was, though, that the straps could not be tied tightly, because they were wet. Thus, we would sometimes watch spellbound as someone jumped into the water and promptly disappeared. The Mae West would float, but the wearer was somewhere beneath it, his presence advertised by the agitation of

With my brother, George, in 1943.

the water as he struggled to get to the surface. The PTI's (Physical Training Instructors) never seemed unduly worried about this, and when the cadet finally surfaced they would merely say that he should have tied the straps more tightly. I finally got my coveted 'X' grading by getting someone else to swim it for me. These irritations aside, ITW was a happy time with a great crowd of cadets. One of them was called Bob Pilkington, one of the Pilkington Glassworks families, and he was a grand friend.

After ITW, we were posted to EFTS (Elementary Flying Training School) at Sywell, near Northampton. Before the war, it had been the home of Brooklands Aero Club. It had evidently been an affluent place, as the original club buildings were used as the Officers Mess, Sergeants Mess and, for a fortunate few, a small mess for cadets. Out of our intake, four of us were selected to use this one, instead of the large, standard type, used by the others. When we first used the mess, I could not believe it. It seated about thirty people, all on pre-war, leather covered, elegant chairs. The tables always had sparkling white tablecloths, and we each had a napkin. The final delight was that we had two civilian waiters to look after our every need. So there we were, receiving three shillings (15p) a day and living like lords. I felt that the RAF was the best thing that had ever happened to me in my life.

We flew Tiger Moths at Sywell, often very badly. To see some long-suffering Tiger with its nose stuck in the ground was such a common sight that it barely warranted a mention. My instructor was a very bad tempered Australian, called Flight Lieutenant Spillman. He hated instructing, and on one occasion was heard to say that he was fed-up with trying to teach kids how to fly, so things did not auger well for me. I found that judging the stall- height when landing was difficult; when taking-off, it was a tricky job to counter the bias of the rudder-bar spring. So, instead of taking-off in a straight line, I tended to do it along a curve. The flight lieutenant would hold his head or thump the side of the cockpit in temper as we performed these undignified manoeuvres. We were expected to go solo within eight hours instruction, and it soon became clear that this was unlikely in my case. Therefore, on one occasion when we were flying along, I said to him,' How about us forgetting the instruction and doing some aerobatics?' To my astonishment, this seemed to please him no end. He became almost friendly as he told me to check that my Sutton Harness was secure, and then proceeded to do loop-the-loops, and generally have a fine time. I thoroughly enjoyed the experience. In the mess during the evening meal, we all roared with laughter as we each recounted the day's latest flying disasters. It was great fun.

One day there was tremendous excitement, when two Flying Fortresses crash-landed on the 'drome. Each had been severely mauled, and there were huge pieces missing from the tail and the wings, plus a liberal sprinkling of holes in the fuselage. I was surprised that they could still fly. Of course, it gave us the chance to scramble all over them. I must confess that they did not seem to be very comfortable aircraft to me, and I had no desire to fly in them. My idea of heaven was to fly in a Lancaster. One of the Fortresses, when it had crashed, had ploughed across the field and ended-up by ramming a white-painted Wellington bomber which had been destined for service with Coastal Command. It had been assembled at the factory at Sywell, and from there would be flown to its squadron. For some reason, it had stood outside the hangers for several weeks, and we had come to regard it as an old friend. When flying, and the instructor told us to fly back to base, one only had to scan the ground to find the white Wellington and fly towards it. Now all this was changed, as both the Wellington and the Fortress were carted away in pieces, much to our dismay. The other Fortress, though, was stripped of non-essentials such as guns and ammunition, and flown back to its base. At the time of take-off, we were all eagerly gathered around to watch the event. However, as the engines were revved up someone yelled, 'Look at the Tigers!' About three of them were parked in a position where they were in the path of the slipstream, and were trying to get airborne. We forgot about the Fortress, and dived across the wings of the Tigers to weigh them down. Finally, the Fortress trundled forward, and in a surprisingly short distance was airborne. I would be eighteen at this time.

At the end of the Grading School course, we waited for the verdict on our flying ability. We all, of course, hoped to be selected for pilot training, although I did not rate my chances very high. In fact, I was selected for navigator training. I was not particularly depressed, as I quickly convinced myself that it would be just as exciting as being a pilot. I reasoned that if you take enough monkeys and give them enough training, then at least one will learn to fly - but will never be able to navigate. My main worry was that I would be posted to Jurby for my training, when what I really wanted was to go to Canada or South Africa. Time alone would tell which it was going to be. Meanwhile, we were all posted to Heaton Park in Manchester.

Heaton Park was the holding unit for all PNB aircrew cadets awaiting further training. We expected to be there for about six weeks. However, there were so many cadets that they could not all be accommodated on the camp. (Fortunately, it did not occur to us to ask WHY they needed so many). Therefore, the cadets of number Three Squadron slept in nearby civilian houses. Accordingly, this was the squadron to be in, but for once, my luck deserted me, and I was allocated to number Two Squadron. Heaton Park had, and I suppose still has, a high wall around the perimeter. It had three gates, where unlucky cadets were on guard duty, so if you returned to camp after hours, you had two ways of getting in. You could just walk up to the gates and the cadets would obligingly let you in. However, if an NCO was present you would be put on a charge. Therefore, to be safe, it was better to scale the wall. This was not difficult, but was a nuisance if it was raining. At one point, the wall obligingly dipped to a height of only about four feet for a distance of three feet. However, this easy access was avoided like the plague, because it was purpose-built to provide easy access to the ESW (Emergency Static Water) tank on the other side of the wall. This was a large, circular tank filled with water to a depth of several feet. Although we almost all knew about it, from time to time some unfortunate newcomer got soaked.

There was a third way of getting into the camp easily, and that was to walk in with number Three Squadron cadets. I often got in this way, as I had become friendly with a charming girl called Muriel Bowler. After the dance at the Middleton Baths, I would walk her to her home in Ivy Drive, which took about ten minutes. Her parents would give me supper, and then make up a camp bed for me to spend the night. By the time that I got back to camp in the morning I just had time to go on parade, so it was too late to return to my billet to make-up my bed. But I did not give it a thought, as I knew that one of the other cadets in the Nissen hut would have done it for me. This was another example of how we all looked after each other's interests. Sometimes only half the beds would be occupied, but those of the missing cadets would be made-up by those left. Often we did not even know who had done it. Aircrew cadets were issued with three bed sheets, a privilege denied to almost all other airmen, so that was nice.

I mentioned my friend Muriel Bowler earlier, and I feel that I should also mention her parents, as they were so kind to me and made me so welcome. Her father had been awarded the Military Cross in the first war, and, when I knew him, he was a major in the Home Guard. He was a kind, but no-nonsense sort of a chap, and we got on well together. Mrs. Bowler was a large and jolly woman. She was even cheerful when she returned from shopping. Shopping at that time consisted mainly of queuing for, perhaps, a half an hour just to get one item. However, although the rations were small, she still insisted that I had meals with them.

On the camp, lavatory verse was common. Although I never subscribed to it, I was nevertheless an avid reader. The scribbling ranged from the elementary:

One would think with all this wit,
Shakespeare himself had been here to sit.

To the much better ongoing ones, such as:

> *Joe for king.*

This referring to Joe Stalin. Underneath was the follow-up:

> *Bing for king.*
> *Joe can't sing.*

Bing referred to Bing Crosby, the crooner. This was followed by:

> *Though, in movements he seems slow,*
> *There's none as quick as good old Joe.*
> *And even though he cannot sing,*
> *We still don't want Bing for king.*

The Station Commander got to know about this graffiti and, to our astonishment and delight, a pompous Daily Routine Order was issued, reminding us that Joe Stalin was a Communist (for the benefit of our dimmer brethren), and that it was seditious to suggest that he could supplant the king. This triggered a renewed bout of scribbling, but sadly the verses became so long and complicated that I can no longer remember them. What happy and irreverent times they were!

Life on the camp was pleasant enough. We attended some token lectures and did a bit of drill, but, largely, we were left to our own devices. Furthermore, our pay was increased from three shillings a day to seven and sixpence (43p) a day. Our pay was the same as that paid to sub-mariners, air gunners and commandos. Dances were available every weekday evening, and I went dancing at the Middleton Baths. It was great fun and, to paraphrase a Prime Minister many years later, we had never had it so good. With the complete disregard for all the terrible things that were going on in the world, that is so common with young people, we felt great to be alive. One of the disconcerting things about our dance partners was that they seemed to know more about where we were to be posted than us. So it was, that one evening my partner asked me how long I had been at Heaton Park. When I told her, she casually informed me, correctly, that I would be sent to South Africa.

To ease the overcrowding at Heaton Park, some of us were posted to operational squadrons for a few weeks. I was sent to Woolfox Lodge, the base of a Short Stirling squadron. The station straddled the A1 road, the accommodation being on one side of the road, and the airfield the other. Soon one of the NAAFI girls took a shine to me. She was a sweet and tender girl called Kathy Allen. In the evenings, when the NAAFI was closed, we would go for a walk, arm in arm, often to watch the bombers taking off on their mine-laying operations. I recall one evening when we were watching them, when she said, 'You will always be careful when you are flying, won't you?' This from a teenager who had already volunteered to go with the NAAFI vanguard to the invasion beaches. I lost contact with her when I left Woolfox Lodge, but I so hope that all went well for that charming girl. The NAAFI girls had to put up with lots of poor-taste jibes from the airmen. For example, they made rock cakes ('Are they made from real rocks?'), tea ('This tea tastes like coffee and looks like cocoa') and similar so-called jokes. The girls took it in good part, which is probably more than I would have done.

I was attached to the armoury section, and the work consisted mainly of loading the aircraft with mines. The load was so heavy that, should an operation be cancelled, we would be summoned by Tannoy at about 10 p.m. to go to the aircraft and unload the mines. Otherwise, the strain would be too great for the undercarriage. The armourers were not bothered whether or not we cadets were present, so we took it in turns to slope off. When it was my turn, I decided to go up to the 'smoke' (London). This was easily done, as the American Air Force base of Cottesmore was about three miles up the road. Consequently, there was a constant stream of traffic along the A1 from the base, so one only had to wait a few minutes to get a lift. In my case, it was in a trailer towed by a Jeep. By the time that we reached Piccadilly, both the jeep and the trailer were full to overflowing with servicemen. That evening I went dancing at the Covent Garden Opera House, so ended up taking a girl home to Dagenham, and an American soldier took her friend home. The girls told us that Dagenham was miles away, but we said that was o.k. It was just as well, for out there we were not asked for our leave passes when we went to a hostel, whereas we would have been had we stayed in Central London.

The next day I hitchhiked back to camp, and arrived at about four o'clock in the afternoon. As soon as I opened the door they said, ' Good Lord, where have you been? We are posted back to Heaton Park tomorrow morning, and we have already had two parades. Fortunately, they did not count us, but merely called the roll, so we were able to answer for you.' It seems that they had telephoned all the likely hostels that they could think of in London to try to contact me. It was yet another example of how everybody looked after everyone else's interest. The camaraderie amongst the cadets was tremendous. That evening I made a point of going to the NAAFI to see Kathy. She had been worried sick, because she knew from the other cadets that I had missed the parades. However, she was soon back to normal when I assured her that all was well. After the NAAFI closed, we went for a stroll as usual, but when we got back she took me into the deserted building to give me a present. She was crying as she handed me a little parcel. It contained a hairbrush and a bottle of hair oil. The girls were only paid a pittance, so it must have been a real sacrifice for her to buy the things. I was very touched by her kindness. I kissed her goodnight, and thought that would be the last that we would see of each other. The next morning, very early, we clambered on to the back of a three-ton lorry for the journey back to Heaton Park. On the way to the station gate we passed the NAAFI, and there was a yell of 'Here she is, Cob!' I was bundled to the tailgate, and there with tears flowing down her face, was Kathy waving goodbye. I waved back, and soon she was lost from view. Dear, sweet Kathy. I prayed that everything would go well for her. I have never seen her from that day to this.

We arrived back at the 'Park, and were given three days embarkation leave. That meant that I arrived in Douglas one day, and two mornings later returned to England. As the girl at the dance had predicted, we were posted to South Africa. We already had a full kit bag each, and we were now issued with a further one, this time full of flying clothing, plus a third, full of tropical kit. Any German spies who had failed to talk to the girls at the dance, merely had to see us staggering under the burden of three kit bags plus a pith-helmet tied to one of them, to make a shrewd guess at our destination. The flying clothing consisted of various items of underwear, boots, gloves and outerwear, plus a leather helmet, goggles and sun glasses. The quality of the kit was surprisingly good. For example, there was a pair of silk long Johns to wear next to the skin. Then came the normal battle dress and over this was a kapok-padded inner overall. On top of this was worn a canvas outer overall, complete with a large fur collar. The flying boots were warm and comfortable, if you did not have to walk in them. However, it quickly became apparent that if you had to bale-out, one sure result of the parachute opening was that you stopped your headlong descent, but your boots just kept going. In an attempt to prevent this, mess-tin straps were fastened tightly around the ankles. I doubt if it did any good, though, as my boots were still a sloppy fit, no matter how tightly the straps were tied. There were four separate pairs of gloves. Silk for next to your skin, then chamois leather, wool and, finally, leather gauntlets. With all of these on it was difficult to write with a pencil or use the navigational computer.

In Scotland, we boarded the Nea Hellas, the New Greece. God alone knows what the Old Greece was like, for this one was a tub. We were allocated hammocks on 'E' deck, just about at the water line. There were no stretchers to be had, so we were doomed to sleepless nights, wrapped like cocoons in the very uncomfortable hammocks. After a week of this torment, several of us decided to move to 'F' deck, where we could sleep on the floor. It was well below the water line, but much more comfortable. We slept there until the ship entered the Red Sea, by which time it was so hot that we slept on deck.

Some enterprising cadets managed to produce a ship's paper during that long voyage, which took us out into the Atlantic, before slipping past Gibraltar at the dead of night to avoid prying eyes. The paper contained an amusing poem, part of which I can still remember:

> *Relax and have a belly laugh*
> *At the foibles of the jolly RAF*
> *Who, suddenly bereft of gin,*
> *Toil not, neither do they spin.*
> *They lounge aboard the Nea Hellas,*
> *Delightful, Brylcreemed, pukka fellas... .*

The reality was that the food was awful, mainly barely edible fish, and nothing to do all day and every day. The horrendous trip took six weeks. However, also in the convoy was an aircraft carrier, which rolled dreadfully the entire voyage, so the sailors in her must have had a terrible time.

Maybe it was just boredom, or maybe it was just devilment, but after a while, as we proceeded down the Red Sea, someone decided to throw his pith helmet overboard. This must have struck a chord, for soon there were dozens of them bobbing about in the ship's wake. By the time that we reached South Africa, I do not think many cadets still had one. Strangely enough, although we had been solemnly issued with them in England, we were never called to account for not having them when we reached South Africa. Another item that we did not have to account for was the tin of emergency rations, which had been issued to each individual. It was just as well, as the food on the ship was so disgusting that we quickly started eating the emergency stuff, particularly as it included a large block of very thick chocolate. So, very soon there were no emergency rations left. I do not suppose the convoy was in much danger from U-boats anyway, as the invasion of Europe had just started, so I expect that they were all busy elsewhere.

At night, it was interesting to stand on deck and practice star recognition. The conditions were perfect, as the black out was rigidly enforced. Whilst in Northern latitudes it was possible to estimate our latitude by reference to the pole star. It got nearer to the horizon as we travelled south, until, finally, it was gone. Now I could see, for the first time in my life, the Southern constellations, such as the Southern Cross and the Scorpion. Finally, the dreadful voyage ended when we docked at Durban. As the ship was being berthed, a woman dressed in white was singing to us from the quayside. She had a lovely voice, and soon many of us were joining in with her. The singing lasted for about a half an hour. I learned later that the singer was known as The Lady in White, and that she was an opera singer. She had made it her voluntary duty to greet every troopship that docked in Durban. After the war, the British Government decorated her for her efforts. Sadly, I recently saw in the paper that she had died.

After wartime Britain, Durban was a fairyland. There was no black out, plenty of beautiful weather, and an abundance of food. In the services canteens the older women prepared the food and the younger ones were keen to be servers. Heaven was never like this! Strangely, though, the food on the camp was not very good. It seems that when the Empire Training Scheme was set up, the provision of cooking facilities was rather overlooked. It did not matter, of course, as we could eat in the many canteens in town. In the camp, we slept on the floor on straw mattresses. The huts had concrete floors and brick walls, but no doors or windows - just open spaces where they should have been. One of the cadets in my hut played the trumpet, and when the flight sergeant heard of it, he ordered him to sound reveille at six o'clock every morning. There was doom and gloom in the hut, because we realised that he would not go outside to make the ghastly noise, but would play it whilst lying in bed, just as any of the rest of us would have done. The following morning we were wakened by this dreadful noise. He got about half way through before the shouts of 'Shut up' and the volley of shoes persuaded him that it was better to endure the wrath of the flight sergeant than of us, and he judiciously stopped playing. As it happened, the flight sergeant slept out of earshot, so we were all happy - he because he thought the noise was being played each day and we because it was not.

Then it was off to Port Elizabeth, where we did concentrated class work. Our Flight Commander was a South African called Captain Long. He always had his dog with him, so quickly they were dubbed Lat and Long (latitude and longitude). Whether he was a poor instructor, or we were poor pupils, the fact was that our flight, 'K' flight, ended the mid-term examinations at the bottom of the pile, with the worst results of the whole squadron. Almost all of us were summoned to appear before the Squadron Commander, a young Australian squadron leader. We expected a real roasting, or even to be told that we had failed the course. We were surprised, therefore, when he breezed into the room and casually sat on one of the tables. He said, "Clearly you're either doing too much studying and not seeing enough of the girls, or the other way round. Whichever it is, change it." That was it. We were dismissed, to our profound relief. However, Lat and Long disappeared from the scene, and we got a new and much better instructor. In fact, in the final examinations 'K' flight came out on top.

One of my friends was the envy of us all, for he knew Vivian Leigh. She had played Scarlet O'Hara in the film 'Gone With The Wind', and we all fantasised like mad about her. He had worked in a bank that she used regularly, and often talked to Jack Hewitt, my friend. I lost touch with him after Port Elizabeth, but I heard that he had been killed in a flying accident shortly afterwards. Up to now we had only flown in Tiger Moths at Grading school, so we looked forward to our next posting. This was to an airfield called Collendale, which was just outside East London. We would fly in Avro Anson's and, if we completed the course, would receive our brevets. The failure rate on each course was invariably quite high, being about fifty per cent. So less than ten cadets received a brevet for every hundred or so that started out. When we arrived at Collondale, we were

This was the only time that I had my photograph taken whilst wearing flying clothing. Here I am with my two friends, Guy Cohen and Don Clifford, whilst under training in South Africa, 1944.

assembled and informed that there were six too many cadets for the course. Therefore, six would have to stay behind and join the next course. As it happened, there were six of us who were good pals, so we decided that if any of us drew a short straw, then we would all stay behind. I was almost the last one to draw, and to my horror, I drew the last short straw. There were loud groans from my friends and much bantering, but without hesitation, every one of them immediately volunteered to stay behind.

It was only for a few weeks, and then we merged with the next course. At last, we were doing some proper flying, and I loved every minute of it - even when winding the undercarriage up by hand. Therefore, it was lessons for half the day and flying, often at night, every day. Night flying was a new and exciting experience for me. The feeling of isolation from the rest of the world as we flew in a black void was a wonderful sensation. Not so wonderful was the necessity to be on parade at seven o'clock each morning for physical training, unless you had been flying the previous night. My friend, 'Colonel' Smith, a university graduate, and I decided to give the P.T. a miss, as the roll call was only made of one flight each time. Thus, we would only be missed about one day in seven. Consequently we would be called before our flight commander every few days to account for our absence. He was unconcerned, and would smile as he told us to run around the block for half an hour. Finally, that wonderful day arrived when those of us who had survived the course were to parade to receive our brevets. The parade was something of a let-down really, as it consisted of the twenty of us sitting in a small hanger, and the Station Commander giving us what he regarded as a pep talk about carrying the war to the enemy. Fighting the enemy had not played much part in our lives up to then, as all that we wanted to do was fly.

I was nineteen when I qualified as a navigator. By that evening we were wearing our sergeant stripes and the coveted navigator brevet, underneath which we all secreted a sixpence piece for some reason that I did not understand, but which I was happy to go along with. About five of the newly qualified aircrew, all tall and powerful looking, still wore their cadet uniforms. They were to be commissioned, and could not get their uniforms until the next day, by which time the rest of us had serious hangover problems. Then it was off to Pretoria with some sight seeing in Johannesburg thrown in. Then came the most memorable flight of my life.

We knew that we were to be posted to the Middle East for our OTU (Operational Training Unit), but we did not know how we would get there. There were two possibilities. We could be flown in Sunderland flying boats, via Lourenco Marques in Mozambique, or else by Dakota transports up the length of British Africa. We hoped for the first, as the stop in Lourenco Marques was in neutral (Portuguese) territory. Therefore, travellers were given cash to buy civilian clothes, and this seemed a super idea. However, instead we were selected to fly from Pretoria to Cairo by Dakota. This, of course, was still marvellous. Before the war, rich people would have paid thousands of pounds to do this same flight with Imperial Airways. So one day we boarded the aircraft for the journey that would take several days. The first leg was to Bulawayo in Southern Rhodesia, then on to Salisbury, Ndola, and so on. I recall Kisumu in Kenya, near Lake Victoria, Khartoum in the Sudan and so to Heliopolis near Cairo. There were some other stopovers that I can not recall. The whole trip was over British or British controlled territory, and I marvelled that this was only a small part of the fabulous British Empire. The organisation was superb, and everywhere was clean, comfortable and peaceful. Each place had a nice lounge and the food was splendid. Add to this that each leg of the flight was a very leisurely affair, and we flew at only about five thousand feet, so the temperature was just right. We had wonderful views of the countryside and the wildlife, and if there was something of particular interest, the pilot obligingly flew low and circled to give us a better look. I shudder to think how much a comparable trip would cost today, and yet here we were being paid to do it. Now that I was a

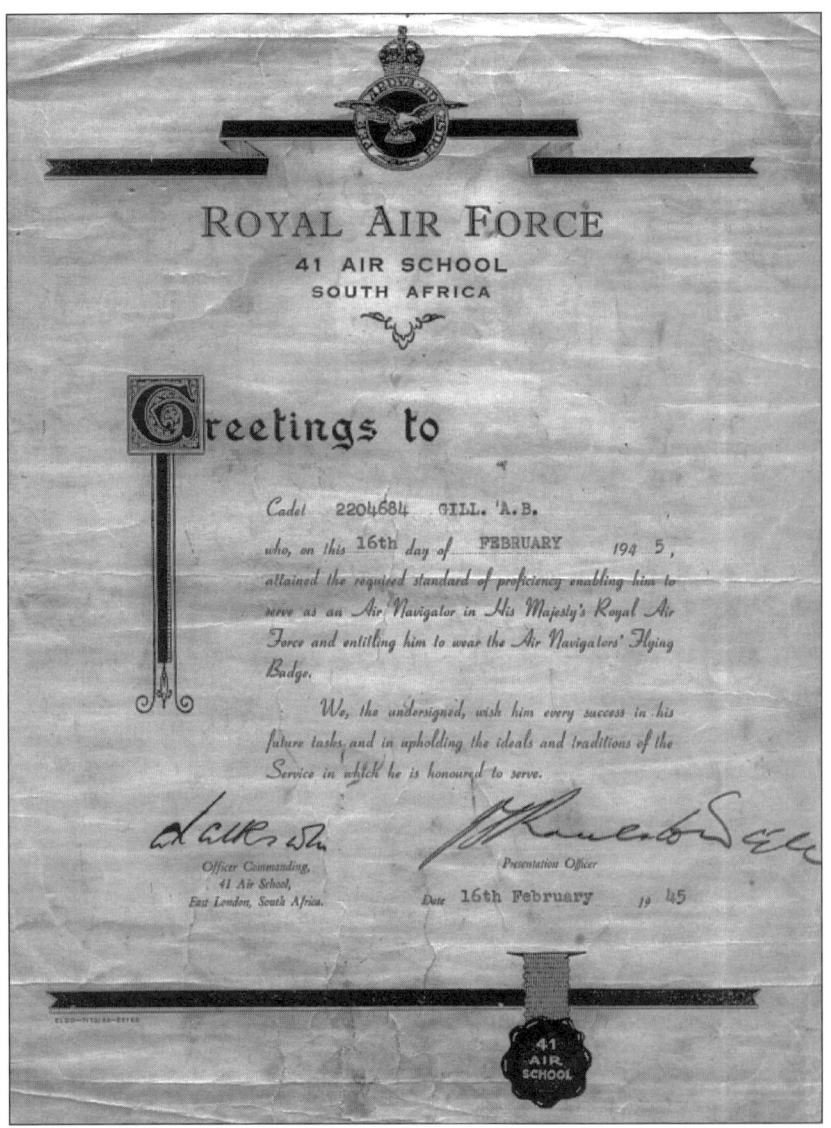

My passing out certificate from 41 Air School. Typically for the RAF, we had to pay 2/6d if we wished to have a certificate.

My brevet at last! This photograph was taken in Tel Aviv, Palastine, whilst I was on leave from my OTU in Qastina, 1945.

sergeant, my pay was 13/6d (65p) a day, so I could live in grand style for a nineteen- year old. At several of the stopovers, we had time to look around, two that I particularly remember being Kisumu and Khartoum. It could not go on forever, of course, and eventually we arrived at Heliopolis, having had a good look at the Pyramids of Giza on the way.

We had several days leave in Cairo, and I spent one afternoon looking around the Cairo Museum. There were not many people in the place, and I was the only person present in the room where Tutunkhamoun's treasure was displayed, apart from two sleepy, armed guards. After the war, the treasure was displayed in London, and people queued for hours to get in. After my leave I was posted to Qastina in Palestine for my O T U. This was a very important posting, for it was here that I would join a crew. It was amazing how many people that I already knew from my various courses. We were given two days to form crews. After that time, anyone left would be allocated to a crew. In my case, it was easy, for Joe Fennell, a bomb aimer whom I had known in South Africa, asked me if I fancied flying with him. I agreed, and that was that. He had already sorted out a pilot and several other crewmembers, so soon we had a full crew. We would be flying Wellington bombers, so there would be seven of us. The skipper was a pilot officer, called Bob Moore. At first, because of his rank, I thought Bob must have only recently qualified as a pilot, but this was not so. It turned out that he had been an N C O instructor at an instructor's training school for some time. His Commanding Officer told him that if he was good enough to teach officers to fly, he was good enough to be an officer himself, and so Bob received his commission. He was about twenty-five, a lot older than the rest of us, as Joe Fennell, and I were nineteen and the gunners, seventeen.

What was the crew like? Well, Bob, besides being a superb pilot, was an excellent leader. He rarely lost his temper and never derided any member of the crew. If he had to tell anyone off, it was

always when only he and the person concerned were alone. For example, we were once flying over the Mediterranean and Bob's voice came on the intercom:
"Pilot to wireless operator. There's an Allied warship ahead, Bill. Fire the colours of the day, please."
"Wireless operator to pilot. Roger".
The colours of the day were various coloured Varey cartridges, and the appropriate colour was changed every hour. Therefore, in his box of six or seven flares, Bill had to select the correct one for that time; but the trouble was that he did not know which it was, as he had fallen asleep during the pre- flight briefing. He hopefully asked me if I knew which it was, but I did not. In desperation he selected a flare at random and fired it. However, his chance of selecting the correct one was not good, and his nerve failed him. He told Bob that he did not know which was the correct colour. Bob, who had been serenely flying towards the warship, let out a yell. The aircraft banked hard to port as he quickly put distance between us and the ship, for even if they thought that we were in an Allied aircraft, they would open fire on us if we failed to fire the correct colour of the day. None of us heard anything more about the incident, but it was certain that Bob would quickly get Bill on his own and give him a real dressing down for his negligence.

As the only officer in the crew, we did not see much of Bob except when flying. He could not invite us to the Officers Mess, and we could not invite him to the Sergeants Mess. What contact that we did have was informal. We never saluted him, and always called him Bob. That was how both he and we wanted it. He did not have much in the way of small talk, his conversation usually being about flying or the crew. If, during a flight, I thanked the rear gunner for obtaining better drifts with his gun-sight than I could with my primitive drift meter, Bob would go out of his way to say he appreciated me involving the gunners in the navigation. We had no second pilot, so the job of assisting Bob fell to the flight engineer, a grand chap called Ben Burliegh. He, along with Joe Fennell, was my particular friend.

Some of the crew at Qastina. Rear: self and Joe Fennell (Bomb aimer). Front: Bill Bateman (Wireless operator) and 'Curly' Elliott (Gunner).

He was the only married man in the crew. He never discussed his home life with us, except to tell us the name of his wife. Like all the other flight engineers, Ben had been a ground fitter before re-mustering to flying duties, so he was a little bit older than the rest of us. Ben left us when we finished at Qastina, although I can not recall on what grounds. My particular friend, though, was the bomb-aimer, Joe Fennell. To this day, I am still in touch with him. He was about five feet-ten inches tall, and the same age as me. He was a kind and quiet man who loved flying. He was an excellent bomb-aimer and map-reader, and he never lost his temper. Nor did his quiet sense of humour ever desert him. He often talked to me about his plans to get married when the war was over to his girl friend, Sylvia, who was serving in the WRNS. He never had the slightest doubt that he would survive the conflict. Joe was an excellent friend - always quiet, calm and unruffled. He did various things to help me whilst we were flying, so we had lots of contact. I always felt completely at ease with Joe and, if I had to confide in anybody, it would have been to him. The wireless operator was Bill Bateman, a happy and carefree eighteen year old Scot. When we were flying, he would be totally engrossed in his wireless world. On the ground he was friendly with everyone, but rather kept to himself. There were three gunners, all of whom were aged seventeen. They were Pete Wilson, 'Curly' Elliot and 'Taffy' Jones. Pete later became a police inspector, and I still have occasional contact with him. They were all grand chaps to have around. So, that was the crew. There was never any backbiting, bad temper or enmity. We all, as far as I could tell, were pleased to be members of such an excellent crew. We would never know how we would have behaved if we had been exposed to enemy attack, for in the event the war passed us by. However, we did not know that at that time. For my part, I could not have been in finer company.

Fighter affiliation consisted of us being attacked by a Spitfire fitted with camera guns. An attack usually commenced with the fighter on the Wellington's beam. When the fighter had closed to cannon-firing range (600 yards), it would have manoeuvred to a position astern of us, and ready to open 'fire'. Acting on the gunner's patter, Bob corkscrewed the aircraft. This involved spiralling almost vertically downward until, when near the ground, the downward motion was stopped. Ben held the rudder bar in the central position, whilst Bob pulled hard on the control column, putting his feet on the dashboard to obtain extra leverage. The aircraft was put into its maximum rate of climb on full power until, when the next attack occurred, the whole procedure was repeated. The sickening dance in the sky continued for about a half-an-hour, and by the end of the time Bob was almost exhausted. The physical effort required of him was considerable. We all knew that this was not a game. With a cannon-firing FW190, our chances of survival would be low. I used to look around the crew and wonder how they would have reacted had the attacks be real. Would anyone have been in a panic? Certainly not Bob. In fact, as far as I could see, none of the others, either. I was the only person that I had any doubt about. Anyway, we would never know, as we were never put in that situation. Normally, Bob insisted on intercom silence except for regulation patter. If you just wanted to chat to someone, you bawled in his ear over the engine noise. The only exception was if I tuned the direction-finding aerial to a station broadcasting dance music, and put it on to the general intercom. for all to hear.

At Qastina, we spent a lot of time on aircraft familiarisation as we were expected to know a host of intimate details about the Wellington, such as changing petrol tanks, the location and operation of various emergency devices, and so on. When we had our individual examinations, I was the only person who obtained full marks. This pleased Bob enormously, as even he only got about 95%. So there we were, a competent and professional crew. We had unquestioning confidence in each of the others, and we were pleased to have such a good skipper. He had no favourites, which was as it should be - everyone was treated with equal respect and friendliness.

On one night flight we did a 'bombing' raid on Cairo (i.e., we took

A B24 Liberator of 356 Squadron, painted by the author. The only Liberator left in the U K is at the Cosford Aerospace Museum.

infra-red photographs of the target), and it was a searchlight affiliation exercise. As we approached the city, the probing fingers from the searchlight batteries got nearer and nearer, until one of them locked on to us. Several others immediately joined it, and we were 'coned'. It was a nightmare for Bob, as he could not see out of the aircraft because of the blinding light. All he could do was keep looking at the instrument panel as he jinked and weaved the aircraft madly, to try to shake off those accursed lights. Jink, twist, weave, turn, everything was to no avail. The cockpit was so brilliantly lit that it hurt ones eyes. The affiliation gave us a valuable insight into the devastating effect of being coned. We had respect for the searchlights afterwards.

At a particular time each day the NAAFI van parked at a spot from which we could get a good view of the runway, so it was pleasant to watch the aircraft landing and taking off. One day, though, it was clear that a Wellington that was landing was in trouble. It was going far too fast when it touched down, and clearly it was going to run out of runway. Sure enough, it was still going fast when it trundled off the end of the runway and onto the waste ground beyond, where it came to rest. Flames were coming from the fuselage, and the crack of exploding ammunition could be clearly heard. All of this was going on whilst we watched fascinated, but still devouring our tea and buns. As soon as the aircraft came to rest, the crew quickly got out. They ran as fast as possible in their cumbersome flying clothing to get clear of the machine in case the petrol tanks exploded. We cheered them on, but were too far away to be able to help. I knew the navigator quite well and when I asked him whether he had been afraid during the incident, he assured me that he had not. He was much more concerned that, during the flight, he had taken his quota of about ten astro-sights. All of them were now lost, so he would now have to do them all again.

On completion of the course, we were to be posted to a squadron in Italy, but this changed when, in May, there was V E Day.

That evening there was a big celebration in the mess, but for some reason, I just wanted to be on my own. I decided to go to the camp cinema. I can not remember what the film was, but I do remember that I was one of the very few people there. Meanwhile, in Hillside Avenue a street party was arranged for the children. It seems that it was a good party, the weather was fine and a good time was had by all. Back in Qastina, our posting was changed to Abu Suir in Egypt, where we were to convert to B24 Liberator bombers. It was a six-week course, and I much preferred flying in Liberators. to Wellington's. We did twelve-hour exercises, usually getting airborne at about three o'clock in the morning. On a typical flight we would fly south to some spot on the Nile, and then turn Northwest across the Qatara Depression to rendezvous with two other aircraft at a place such as Solum, Mersa Matruh or Tobruk. From there, the three of us would fly to Cyprus and then to the live bombing range at Cairo. Once, when I was the lead navigator, the bombs fell just four seconds late after a twelve-hour flight. On another occasion we rendezvoused with two South African crews, one of who was the lead bomb-aimer at the bombing range. The idea was that, when the lead man said, "Bombs gone", all three aircraft dropped their bombs. However, on this occasion Joe did not release our bombs because he said that they would miss the target by miles. Bob was not too pleased with this, as we were obliged to go round again. When we landed, he stalked off to his de-briefing in something of a temper. When he re-appeared, though, he was all smiles, for he had learned that the South Africans had missed the target by a long way and had almost bombed a village by mistake. Joe became the hero of the hour in Bob's eyes.

On another exercise we flew Northwest across the desert and rendezvoused with two other aircraft at Solum at dawn. Sunrise over the desert was a spectacular sight as we approached the port. I was always amazed at the scale of destruction of places such as this, although the war had passed it by some time before. The buildings were in a sad state, and the harbour was littered with sunken ships.

As if by magic, the other two aircraft appeared and we set off for Cyprus in formation. We were the lead aircraft for the leg. We set course in grand style, but the pilots of the other two aircraft became bored. To while away the time, they gradually eased their wingtips nearer and nearer to the fuselage of our 'plane, so much so that they were getting dangerously close. Bob ordered the pilots away, but they just grinned and kept the aircraft where they were. Bob became annoyed, and after a while he dropped our plane out of the formation and re-formed behind the other two. He said later that flying was dangerous enough, without doing stupid things. I suppose he was right, but I must say that I quite enjoyed our little bit of close formation flying. It had added a little bit of spice to a long exercise. The flying weather was usually good, so navigation was easy. We normally flew at less than ten thousand feet, so it was comfortably warm and we had no necessity to wear oxygen masks. Also, we used throat microphones, and these are much more comfortable than the standard RAF type incorporated into the flying helmet.

One of the not-so-good things about the Liberator, was that the bombs were stored inboard, with a ten inch catwalk between the bomb racks. Therefore, this was a very weak part of the aircraft, so if the plane ditched, it almost invariably broke its back and sank immediately. We, therefore, had a personal stake in practising our ditching drill until we could do it at lightening speed. In fact, we set the record for the station, although it probably would still not be fast enough if we really had to do it.

However, baling-out was a different thing altogether, as there were plenty of places from which to jump. Joe and I shared the nose compartment, so our exit was via the open nose-wheel doors. When the wheel was retracted, there was a large opening through which to get out. It was a common sight near the airfield to see wrecked and burning Liberators. Our course lasted six weeks, and in that period, there were about eight crashes near the airfield. Each aircraft had a crew of nine, and often there were several instructors on board, so the loss of life was quite high.

Upon completion of the course, we were told that we would be posted to ACSEA.

"Where is that?" we enquired.

"Air Command, South East Asia" was the reply.

We were to be flown to India in a Sunderland, but at the last moment, we were told that a Liberator had been flown to Cairo from the USA, and we had been selected to fly it on to India. We were each issued with a Smith and Wesson revolver, as we would be flying over some hostile territory. However, I do not know how we would have fared if we had to use them, as we had not fired a revolver since ITW days. Furthermore, our aiming had been so poor that, back at Scarborough, we used to say that you were safe so long as they were aiming at you. However, it was something of a novelty to wear the gear, and it looked quite smart and workman-like.

We did not have a particular time to get to India, so we planned a nice, lazy, schedule consisting of several short legs, the first being to Tel Aviv in Palestine. We stayed there for several days, before going on to Shieba. This was a notorious RAF station in Persia. In fact, there was a bawdy song called the Shieba Blues, about the heat, dirt and boredom of the place. We arrived one evening, and departed the following morning en route to Karachi in India, and from there to Phaphmou in central India. As we left the aircraft, one of the ground crew told us that the Americans had dropped an atomic bomb on Hiroshima, a place that we had never heard of, in Japan. We thought that the atomic bomb was probably an extremely powerful version of large bombs, such as Tallboy or Grand Slam. It was only when we talked about it in the mess that we learned just how devastating it was, and that it was almost certainly a war-winner. It was strange really, as for the whole time that we had been in the service it had been taken for granted that we would end up in the war that would go on for another one or two years. Now, suddenly, the war had passed us by. We had spent all this time training for something which no longer existed, as everyone agreed that the new weapon meant that the war was won. Even when we learned just how devastating these bombs were, I did not hear anyone saying what 'ghastly' weapons they were. On the contrary, the only thoughts ran along two lines: firstly, that the Japs. had it coming to them, and secondly that the anticipated huge loss of Allied lives when invading Japan would not now materialise. It transpired that it was estimated that there would be over a million Allied casualties. It was many years before I heard the first talk of how inhumane it had been to bomb Hiroshima and Nagasaki.

From Phaphmou we proceeded, via Poona, to Group Headquarters in Ceylon for our posting. It was to join 356 Squadron on the Cocos Islands. As soon as Bob told us, we asked where they were. He explained that they are about half way to Australia, made of coral and form a circle three miles in diameter. They are three feet above sea level, and there is no other land for hundreds of miles. He finished by saying, "If you miss them, Cob, we will not have enough petrol to get to Australia." I thought about it for a while, and said that it would involve flying over nothing but water for about sixteen hundred miles and aiming for a three-mile group of islands. There was no radar there, so it would be just like pre-war navigation, and would take about ten hours. When I look back, I was completely relaxed about the whole thing, particularly as, if we did get lost, we would be in a bit of a predicament. I had just turned twenty, so was quite an old hand by then. None of us had any worries about the trip, and it was never mentioned again.

We were to fly from RAF Kankasanturi, always referred to as KKS. It is at the northern-most tip of Ceylon, very close to a sleepy little town called Jaffna. This was Tamil country, and in recent years, that sleepy town has been the scene of dreadful rioting and killing. To my mind, some of the benefits of the British Empire were that it brought peace, order, prosperity and safety to such places. On the evening before we

The Liberator crew at Poona, India. Bob is in the middle, Joe Fennell is on the right and I am on the left.

were scheduled to take off, Bob, the flight engineer and I inspected the aircraft. I was standing in the bomb bay when I noticed a drop of condensation on the bulkhead. I did not regard it as important, but mentioned it to Bob, anyway. He clambered up to have a closer inspection, smelled it, and said, "It's petrol!" The matter was reported immediately, with the result that the flight was cancelled whilst the leak was repaired. It turned out to be quite serious, and necessitated changing the affected tank. Liberators have five petrol tanks in each wing, and the damaged one was that nearest the wingtip, so all five tanks had to be removed. First, the three thousand gallons of 100-octane aviation fuel already in the tanks, had to be pumped out before work could even begin. The job took about two weeks to complete, and for that time, we lived the life of Riley. We had no work to do, so each day we had transport laid on to take us to the beach. There were also other crews waiting to join the squadron, and one early morning one of them took off. However, the pilot had forgotten to remove the cover from the Pitot tube, and the Liberator was roaring down the runway before he realised his mistake. Instruments, such as the altimeter and the airspeed indicator depend upon the Pitot tube, so he could not possibly proceed. Neither could he land, as he had three thousand gallons of fuel on board. Instead, he was obliged to circle over the sea for hours to use up petrol, before landing. We all thought it was a huge lark.

Finally, our repairs were completed, and we took off at dawn, one bright and sunny morning. I recall watching Ceylon slipping behind us. Joe had fixed the point at which we crossed the coast with ease, as usual. He was a superb map-reader. Then we were over the sea, flying at five thousand feet. After leaving the coast behind, the only crewmembers, beside myself, that had duties to perform were Bill Bateman, (the wireless operator) and Bob. Soon, the sandman had crept up on the rest of the crew, and they were asleep. Bob put the aircraft on automatic pilot, leaned back in his seat, put his feet up on the instrument panel, and pulled his cap low over his eyes. In this seemingly leisurely manner, we continued Southeast for hour after

Bob in the 'office' of Glamour Girl, one of the 356 Squadron Liberator's.

hour. There is no land between Ceylon and the Cocos Islands, so it was impossible to obtain a visual fix. Also, there was no radar, and radio bearings were unobtainable for most of the journey. A further complication was that obtaining astro-sights of the sun only yielded position lines, not fixes, so were only of limited use. However, for just a fleeting second, it was possible to obtain a fix from a particular observation. The angular altitude of the sun increases until, at about mid-day, it is at its maximum. At that moment, the sun is crossing the observer's longitude. Technically, this is known as the Meridional Passage, or Mer Pass, of the sun. Therefore, I would keep the sun in the sight of my sextant, until it reached its Mer Pass. I carefully noted the time and the sun's angular altitude. From the altitude, I calculated our latitude, and from the time, I calculated our longitude. In this manner, I obtained the only fix possible on that long journey.

After about ten hours, with all the optimism of youth, I told Bob that the ETA (Estimated Time of Arrival) was in ten minutes. Bob posted the crew to their lookout stations, for he did not want the Islands to slip past unnoticed. The ETA arrived, with no sign of the Islands. A very long ten minutes later there was still no sign. I decided that I had better start unpacking my gear, when Bob's voice came over the intercom. He said quietly, "There it is, straight ahead. Good show, Cob". This was praise indeed. So, we landed at this remarkable RAF outpost. It had a metal runway so, as we landed, it sounded as though the tail unit had fallen off. The Control Tower had a board fastened on the front, as was normal practice out there, giving the name of the station and the height above sea level - in this case it read, 'COCOS 3 FT'

It seems that being a mere ten minutes late was much better than the average, so we were pleased at the manner of our arrival. We were to fly between Ceylon and the Islands many times later, usually much closer to the ETA, but the trips lacked the excitement of that first time. I loved flying, and hoped that it could go on forever. Bob had tried to get me to let him put me forward for a commission, but I refused. He did not know why, of course, but I was afraid that it would entail another ear test. He also used to urge me to have a go at flying the Liberator. This I was keen to do, but I always seemed to be too busy. Anyway, there was no rush, as we were flying regularly, so there would be plenty of opportunities to come. At this time, my pay was eighteen shillings and sixpence (90p) a day, which included Japanese Campaign Pay.

Life on the island was good. We slept three in a tent, but the weather was generally good, so that was no hardship. The food was almost all tinned stuff, but very good. Rum rations were issued on the slightest pretext so, needless-to-say, we often went to bed in a very happy state of mind. The natives had the skin colour of Indians, but the appearance of Chinese. They were polite and gentle, and lived on Home Island, whereas the RAF Station was on West Island. Home Island was out of bounds to the RAF personnel, but the natives could visit the RAF on Sundays. There had been so much bartering done with the natives, that something of a role reversal had taken place. Many of them proudly wore their RAF blue uniforms, which had been exchanged for chickens and eggs. In addition, as the natives went fishing for days at a time, they had quickly realised the value of items such as the Thermos flasks, which were issued to aircrew, and service pullovers. In fact, the natives were better dressed than we were. The rulers were the Clunies-Ross family, originally from Scotland. Queen Victoria granted them the 'kingdom' of the islands. The natives could leave the islands at any time they wished, but could never return. This was because the place was free of many diseases, such as VD, and Clunies-Ross was determined to keep it that way. The currency consisted of bone coins, one of which I still have. The group of islands was made of coral, so the formation was that of a typical coral atoll. They form a circle, and the water around them is about two feet deep. It extends about a hundred yards offshore to the reef and beyond that you are in the Indian Ocean, so the water is very deep. A couple of aircrew were swept over the reef and drowned, whilst I was there. Fresh water was a very scarce commodity, so there were no showers or wash basins. For washing or sponging down, we each had our tin hat mounted upside down on sticks.

About once a week, a film was shown, the projector being mounted on the back of a lorry, and the screen was held in position with guy-ropes. Therefore, with this arrangement, you could view the screen from the front or the rear. As the start time drew near there was a steady stream of officers and men looking for a good spot to sit, each carrying a stool or box. One film was Blithe Spirit, starring Rex Harrison. Elvira, the blithe spirit of the title, always wafted in on a breeze, and she was making one of her entrances when the screen blew down. The timing was perfect, and we howled with laughter.

When you signed on for aircrew duties, you undertook to do two tours of thirty operations with a six-month break between each tour. This did not seem very demanding when I signed on or, I suppose, to most of the others. It was, of course, naieve of us to think that we would be let off so lightly. Firstly, if you survived the various training courses, it was mathematically impossible to complete even one tour of operations if the average loss rate was more than three aircraft out of a hundred. It was said that, in Europe, if you survived the first five operations, your chances of survival were doubled. The average life expectancy of aircrew was six weeks. Then there was the definition of an operation. A raid on Berlin counted as one, but a mine-laying trip only counted as a third, so it could take a long time to complete an operational tour - and six months later it started all over again. More than fifty-five thousand aircrew were killed. In addition, no matter how close you were to completing a tour, if you refused to fly (and you could do this at any time) you were graded LMF. This was Lack of Moral Fibre. You were stripped of your rank and lost your brevet. You could then expect to be allocated to menial duties such as latrine cleaning. Psychologists were in short supply, so mentally distraught, very young men in aircrew uniform were treated in this way without compunction. There were no counsellors for them. I feel that the crews in the European theatre had the worst time of it.

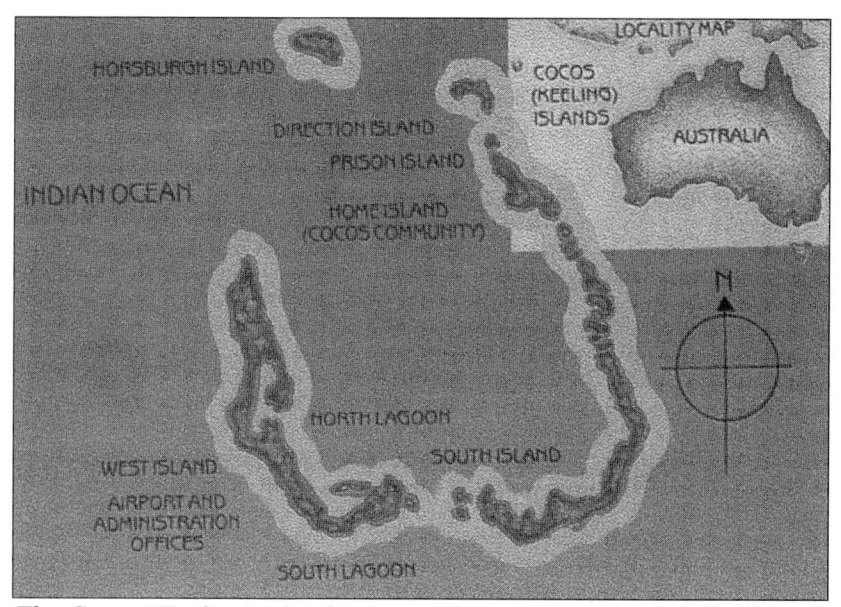

The Cocos (Keeling) Islands, three miles across and three feet above sea level.

Promotion was rapid. After six months on an operational squadron, sergeants became flight sergeants, and six months later they became warrant officers. Also, if you completed a tour you could expect to be awarded a Distinguished Flying Cross if an officer, or a Distinguished Flying Medal if an NCO.

On the Cocos Islands the football pitch was on coral, and as you approached the deserted pitch there were many thousands of land crabs covering the surface. However, as soon as the first person set foot upon the ground, the crabs sank into the coral, so that in less than a minute there was not one to be seen. The economy of the islands depended upon copra from the extensive coconut plantations, and I understand that Clunies-Ross received five pounds compensation for every tree felled for the RAF.

Once, we were flying ground crews to Ceylon on their way home for demobilisation. They were seated in the bomb bay on makeshift seats, from which they had no view out of the aircraft. As we were ready to touch down at Colombo airport they became excited, and rushed to the beam gun positions for a good view, with the result that, instead of his usual immaculate landing, Bob could had to struggle to get the nose-wheel on the ground. He was summoned to the Control Tower to explain his undignified landing, so he was furious. Only once before had I seen him so angry. This was during a flight to the Cocos. We had just come out of briefing, early one morning, when I was approached by two flight lieutenants who wanted a lift to the Cocos, and from there they would go on to Australia on leave. I referred them to Bob, who said that he would be glad to take them. After we had been airborne for several hours, I looked for my lunch box, but I could not find it. Bob said that he knew where it was, but it had gone. Suddenly he remembered the two passengers. He went aft, and sure enough, there they were eating my sandwiches. Bob was incandescent with rage. He said he would charge them with stealing rations when we reached the Islands, but I do not know whether he did.

The Liberator had four Pratt and Whitney 1200 horse power engines, and a gross weight of over thirty tons, with a wing span of 110 feet so it was quite a large aircraft. It was my workplace, and I was, therefore, shocked when, suddenly, my flying was over. It happened without any warning whatever. I was in my tent one morning when Bob appeared. He said that my name had been drawn in the Mid-Tour Leave raffle, and I was to leave the Island in a couple of days. Mid-Tour Leave was granted to a lucky few if their names were drawn in a regular raffle at Headquarters, and guaranteed the winners at least six weeks home leave. To qualify you had to have served overseas for at least eighteen months (i.e., a half of an overseas tour of three years), but even so, the large number of people who were eligible meant that your chances were so small that few people even thought about it. That is how it was in my case. Actually, I was quite contented where I was, so I asked Bob if I could refuse it, but he said that was not possible. Therefore, a little reluctantly, I set off for my leave. I flew as a passenger in Liberators all the way to the UK, never to see the Cocos Islands again.

I was given ten weeks leave in the Isle of Man, so it gave me a chance to catch up with some of my buddies for the first time since joining the RAF. In addition, it was nice to be able to wear civilian clothes again. It was back to the Villa Marina and what was left of the old crowd. The trouble with ten weeks leave, though, is that at the end of it you do not want to go back. I was still receiving eighteen shillings and sixpence a day, so I had lots of money, lots of friends and the home comforts. It was a sad day, therefore, when I received a telegram ordering me to report for duty. I had entertained a vague hope that the RAF may have forgotten me. I was to return to India by sea aboard the Empress of Scotland (formerly the Empress of Japan). Six of us were aircrew, so we shared a very large cabin and dined on our own. We had an airman to wait on us, so we had no cause for complaint. Of the six of us, three were pilots, one of whom came from Colby. His name was Allan Costain, and he flew Spitfires. After the war, he married Dorothy Chalk, who was the best friend of my

Six of us shared a cabin on the Empress of Scotland, when returning from Mid-Tour leave. This photograph was taken in Port Said. Second right is Allan Costain from Colby. He later married my future wife's best friend, Dorothy Chalk. I am third from the left.

future wife. The voyage was very pleasant, and took us past Gibraltar, the second time for me, and again I did not see it, as it was the dead of night. There were many Italian prisoners of war on board. (I expect they were still POW's, although their government had declared war on Germany. At any rate, they were treated as such).

They were disembarked at Naples, and the city was a shambles. The harbour was littered with sunken ships and, in fact, we were moored to some upturned vessels, which were used as a makeshift pier. On the far side of the harbour were some capital ships of the Italian navy. I thought they looked both formidable and beautiful. Every building that could be seen had been destroyed, only their skeletons remaining. That of the dome of the Opera House dominated the scene. It must have been a sad homecoming for the Italians. However, there was a military band there to greet them, and many were met by relatives. Two days later the ship sailed. We were heading for the Suez Canal; but first we passed through the Straits of Messina, and had a delightful view of Stromboli, an active volcano. The larva poured down to the sea in a continuous stream, amazingly close, it seemed to me, to clusters of houses. Then it was on to the canal, the huge statue of Ferdinand de Lesseps standing guard at the entrance. A few days later we docked at Bombay. Here I learned that 356 Squadron had been disbanded, and that most of the aircrews were now mis-employed at RAF Yelahanka, near Bangalore. The NCO aircrew had been before a Redundancy Panel, who had formally declared that they could no longer fly, so were then classed as mis-employed. Although they could retain their rank and pay, they were obliged to cover their badges of rank during working hours, so effectively they were classed as airmen. They were also to be re-trained as, for example, transport drivers, admin staff and so on. However, by the time that I arrived at Yelahanka the Redundancy Panel had moved on. Therefore, I could not be declared redundant, and so I retained my rank of flight sergeant. I still had to be mis-employed, though, so I was put in charge of the Ration Stores. Almost every job on the station was being done by ex-aircrew, but my old crew was not there. However, it was nice to be on friendly terms with everyone from the Station Adjutant down. There was, of course, a sprinkling of officers and NCO's other than ex-aircrew, and one of them was a particularly nasty bit of work. He was a warrant officer in the transport section. We detested him and he reciprocated our sentiments. However, he had no influence, as we held all the key positions. However, he turned out to be a valuable asset to us.

There was a big army presence in Bangalore, and the Military Police there had a fine time making life a misery for the aircrew lorry drivers. The drivers would usually drive without headgear, and would duly be charged with being improperly dressed by the Redcaps. It meant nothing, of course, as the charges were put straight in the bin, but it was annoying. However, retribution was at hand. I suppose it was inevitable that eventually the Redcaps would mistake our Mr Nasty for just another aircrew driver. He was driving without his cap on, when two Redcaps stopped him. They ordered him out of his cab and had a fine time belittling him. They put him on a charge and, laughing, got astride their motor cycles. Mr Nasty had said nothing up to this point, but now he called them both back, stood them to attention and threw the book at them. Finally, he dismissed them. Much subdued, they climbed on to their machines, when Mr Nasty told them that if they attempted to ride their machines whilst improperly dressed (they should have been wearing crash hats) they would wonder what had hit them. He told them to walk their motor cycles back to their base. To make sure they did, he followed them. From then, every Redcap wore a heavy crash helmet, and left the aircrew alone.

In India, the various trades are 'Wallah's'. Thus, the barber is the nappi wallah; the tailor, the derzi wallah; the laundreyman, the dhobi wallah and so on. I have probably spelled the names wrongly, as they are Hindi words. However, the char wallah was rather special, as he sold tea. The tea, or char, was in a large, brass urn, and usually tasted disgusting. However, as he only charged two annas for a large mug of tea, he had a ready sale. He had to put up with a lot of banter, such as, 'You've left the Brasso tin in the urn.' and similar stuff. Having got the tea, the customers signed the char wallah's book so that he could collect his money on pay-day. On payday he would appear, and ask where this sahib was, pointing to a name in the book. The names included Winston Churchill, General Montgomery, Betty Grable, Mickey Mouse and various other fanciful names. I do not know how the char wallah made a profit, but, as he continued to hawk his tea at least for the whole time that I was there, he must have managed it somehow.

    One day Tex Chew, the Catering Officer, said that an Air Commodore would be visiting the station. He would be having dinner, so it must be special. Tex was to go to the market the next day, and when he had decided what the meal would be he would let me know. I would then type the menu cards. He telephoned me at mid-day with the information and said that he would not be back at the office that day. I set about typing the menus, but stumbled when I got to the sweet. Tex had said that it would be meringue, but I suddenly realised that I did not know how to spell it. I telephoned the cooks, but, to my surprise and consternation, none of them knew either. I began telephoning everyone that I knew, with ever - increasing desperation creeping in, as I realised that nobody that I knew could spell that accursed word. I could have resolved the problem by just typing DESSERT, but that seemed an admission of defeat. The deadline was fast approaching, so I took my courage in my hands and typed MERANG. From my recent experience I reasoned that the people at the dinner could not spell it either. The next morning Tex came into the office. "Now then, flight, how do you spell meringue?" I groaned and told him what had happened. Tex roared with laughter and said, " The Air Commodore thought it was a huge joke, and said that whoever had typed the menus had been in the jungle too long, and should be sent home for immediate demob."

    My two particular friends at this time were air gunners, who

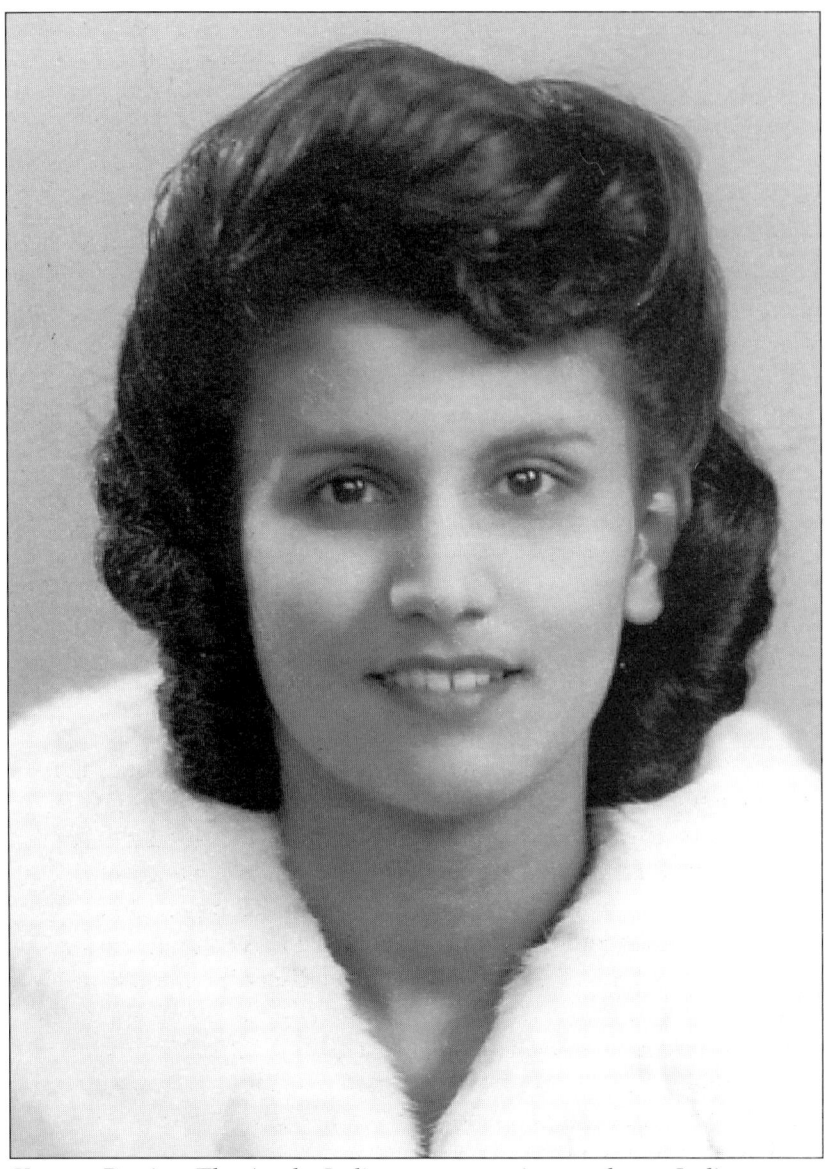

Yvonne Davies. The Anglo-Indians were anxious to leave India, as independence was looming. I have no idea whether Yvonne managed it.

now ran the post office. They had a little van in which to collect the mail from town, so each Sunday morning the three of us drove to Bangalore, as there was a dance held there from ten o'clock until one. After the dance we would go for lunch and then to the cinema. It was at one of the dances that I became friendly with Yvonne Davies, a beautiful Anglo-Indian of my age. She was an intelligent girl and charming company, although for me, she was never more than a friend. However, for her it was potentially much more serious than that. Indian independence was already scheduled for the near future, so the privileged position of the Anglo's would probably disappear. Understandably, they all wanted to get out of India, and the place that they wanted to go to was the UK. However, they could only do that if they married a UK national. So, whilst I was looking for friendship, she was looking for marriage. Yvonne quickly had me home to meet her parents, and she was so keen on hotting-up our relationship that I thought it best to get out. We remained friends, but soon she was involved with a soldier. There were so many girls in Yvonne's situation that it was inevitable that some men took advantage of their position and promised the girls everything, only to abandon them when it was convenient.

 I had my twenty-first birthday whilst I was at Yelahanka. It was not a big deal, for I only received one card. It was from my dear friend Muriel Bowler whom I had met whilst at Heaton Park. Muriel and I remained very good friends until her death in 1996, and I still have and treasure that card. Soon after, it was time to proceed to Bombay for embarkation. There we could abandon any surplus khaki drill clothing. I can still see the huge pile of discarded clothes, and I expect some enterprising Indian made a small fortune selling it at the market. I groaned when we were told the name of the ship that would take us home - the Nea Hellas, the same rust bucket that had taken us to South Africa. This time the trip was a little better, but still not good. After about three weeks, we sailed up the Clyde. How nice it was to be back in wonderful, worn out, Britain again. I feel the poet had it just about right, when he wrote:

> *Breathes there a man with soul so dead,*
> *Who never to himself hath said,*
> *'This is my own, my native land'?*

The port side of the ship was lined with factories, and the starboard side with lush, green fields. Young girls waved and cheered from the factories as we sailed past, and so many of us crowded to the port side that the ship had a list. The captain appealed over the Tannoy for us to look at the beautiful view on the other side, but we were already looking at the most wonderful sight that we could imagine, so the ship proceeded on its lop-sided way up the river.

My days in the RAF were now numbered, and it was with a mixture of happiness and sadness that I reported to Kirkham, near Blackpool, for my demobilisation. The procedure was quick and efficient, and we could select a complete civilian outfit as well as keeping one uniform. Then I stopped off at my Aunt May's in Preston for a few days, where I was pleased to meet up with my cousin George, who had been taken prisoner at Dunkirk. His sister, Dot, was married to a Canadian captain and their elder brother was home from a prisoner of war camp. The blackout was over, and there seemed to be a bright, new future for all of us. So, then it was on to that bittersweet journey home to the Island - happy to be going home, but sad to be leaving the RAF. I think the ship was the Victoria. We sailed past the Tower of Refuge where the Mona had been high and dry, past the end of the Battery Pier where the ghosts of laughing children waved to us, past the Croagh where the flying boat had been moored, and so to our berth at the Victoria Pier. Home again. Now I would go back to Lawton's and become an apprentice again. Whatever the future had in store for me, it could never hope to compete with the excitement and thrills of the life that I was leaving behind. On the ship I had been talking to a merchant seaman from Douglas called Eric Cain. He had sailed in oil tankers across the Atlantic during the war, when he was only sixteen. His sister was the girl I had met at the Villa Marina in 1941, and I enquired whether she had yet been

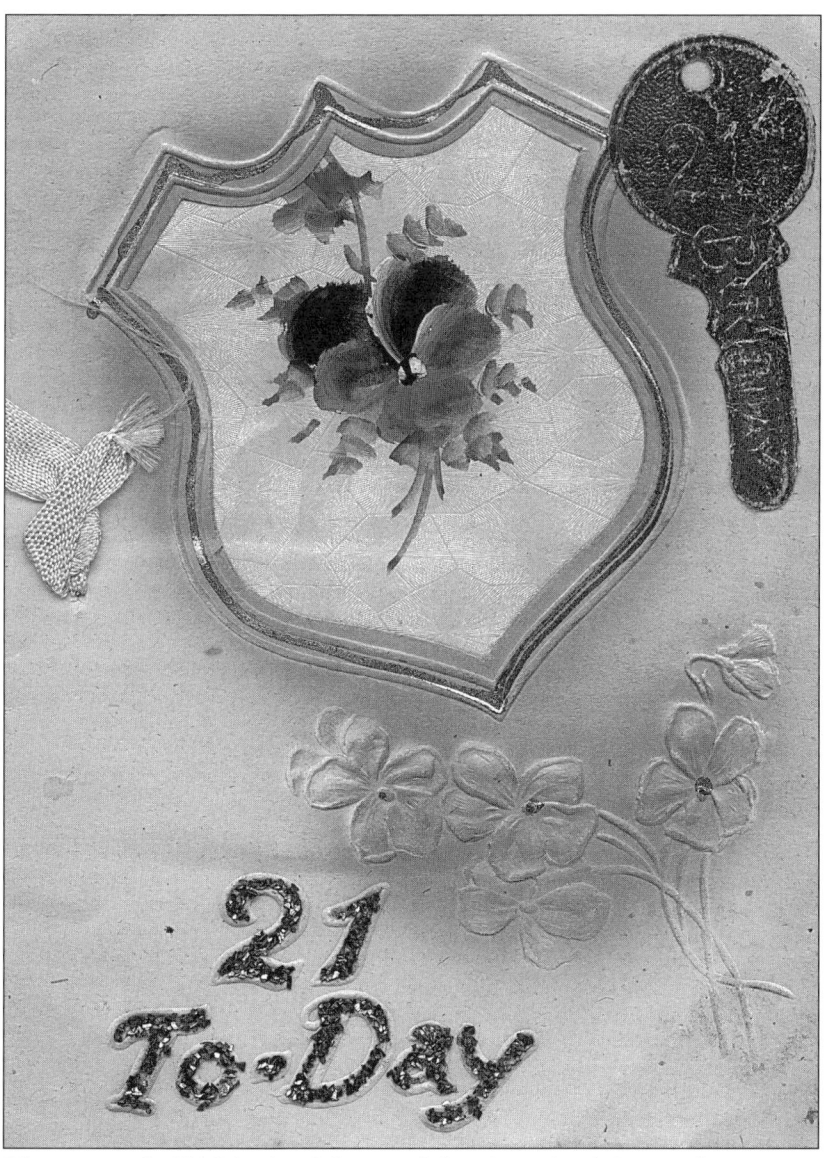

The one and only 21st birthday card that I received. It was from my dear friend, Muriel Bowler.

I married 'Pat' Cain on October 18th 1949. Those present included, L to R: Eric Cain, Arnold Breadner (from the Marine Hotel, Peel- Best Man), Mother, Pat, self, Dad and June Simmons (Bridesmaid). George Broad was the organist for the ceremony.

demobilised. He said she was, and that was that. A few days later I met her in Strand Street, we got chatting and, to cut a long story short, we married in 1949. Her real name is Esther Laura, but in the WAAF, they had called her Pat, and this name stuck. One of her close friends during her time in the WAAF had been a wireless operator/air gunner, called Alec Seymour. He flew in Halifax bombers, and he was killed in the last week of the war.

It was about this time that someone said to me that it was unheard-of for an elementary-school boy to become a pilot, navigator or bomb aimer. Whether this was true or not, I can not say, but, upon reflection, all the people that I had served with were from high school, grammar school or university, so maybe I had been even luckier than I thought.

So that is an outline of my life up to 1947. It had been a happy and, from time to time, an exciting one. The war, although terrible for so many people, was the means by which I realised my ambition to fly, so I had been one of the lucky ones.

It was now time to take stock of who had survived and who had not. Les Hewitt (aircrew), Stan Quine (army), 'Cap' Cain (army), Eric Teare (Guards, and at Monte Casino), Bruce Bridson (merchant navy), Cliff Young (Fleet Air Arm) and others were OK. Fine young men; such as Harold Jergusson (aircrew), Harry Kewley (aircrew), and Doug Hughes (army) were not. My brothers, other than Ernie, had survived the war. George's ship, HMS Cape Siretoko, had been sunk in a Norwegian Fjord on April 28th 1940. The crew was machine gunned as they swam for the shore. He, and the remnants of the crew, tramped overland to a port where the last Allied ship, HMS Glasgow, was about to sail. It was there to take the Norwegian Royal Family to safety. On the way, they sailed near the scene of the loss of HMS Glorious, which was sunk by the Scharnhorst. Had they gone to the assistance of Glorious they would certainly have joined her tragic fate. Presumably, they did not, because of the Royal party on board.

A couple of years later he and a companion were walking down a road in Lowestoft, when a German aircraft flew in from the sea and bombed the area. George was wounded and his companion killed. My other two brothers, like me, had a comparatively uneventful war. My contribution had been so small that I did not have the nerve to apply for the two medals to which I was entitled, the War Service and the Victory Medal, known in the service as the NAAFI and Spam medals. I finally obtained them in 1996 so that my son Quintin could have them. He has told me that he will one day pass them on to his eldest daughter, along with an explanation of how they come to be in our family.

It was nice to renew old acquaintances again, and the sense of elation that we felt can not be imagined now, as we were on top of the world. We had won the war and would remain a World power for far into the future. Food rationing continued and, in fact, it became worse, but the lights were on again and peace had finally arrived. The country was exhausted but triumphant. Everything was wonderful. How could we know that the reality was that the country was bankrupt, and that the Empire was in its death throes? Nevertheless, for a short, blissful period, we had the illusion that everything was back to normal. The Island was bursting at the seams with holidaymakers, the old atmosphere of fun and gaiety was back, and it was good to be alive. Meanwhile, matrimony was claiming the old gang, and in 1949 it would claim me, too.

EPILOGUE

This has been a brief look at my early life. It was a good time, filled with many happy memories of grand people and exciting happenings. For the most part money was in short supply, but this was compensated-for in abundance by the love and companionship that was all around. Regrets are few, but some are painful. For example, my father asked very little from me in return for the splendid way that he helped me on so many occasions, but even so, I failed him. On one occasion, when I was home on my Mid-Tour leave, he asked me to meet him outside the Douglas Courthouse, where the Military Tribunal met. He wished to introduce me to the High Bailiff. I think he was very proud of me, and it would have cost me nothing more than a little of my time. However, I could not conceive that anyone could be that interested in me, so, to my eternal shame, I did not bother to turn up. The beautiful words of Omar Khayyam sum up my feelings so well:

> *The Moving Finger writes; and, having writ,*
> *Moves on: nor all thy Piety nor wit*
> *Shall lure it back to cancel half a line,*
> *Nor all thy Tears wash out a word of it.*

Many of the things that I have mentioned in the book are probably still in common use today, such as, I expect, the skipping songs. On the other hand, I hope that there is sufficient here that is either new or, perhaps, had been forgotten, to make the book of some interest. Most of all, I trust that the three beautiful young girls for whom it was specially written will feel, when they are old enough to read it, that they can relate it to their lives and, maybe in time, their children's lives.

Allan Gill,
Burton-on-Trent, 1999.